IMAGES
of America

STEREOSCOPIC VIEWS
OF THE
WHITE MOUNTAINS

IMAGES
of America

STEREOSCOPIC VIEWS
OF THE
WHITE MOUNTAINS

Bruce D. Heald, Ph.D.

ARCADIA
PUBLISHING

Published by Arcadia Publishing
Charleston, South Carolina

Library of Congress Catalog Card Number: 00-106500

For all general information contact Arcadia Publishing at:
Telephone 843-853-2070
Fax 843-853-0044
E-mail sales@arcadiapublishing.com
For customer service and orders:
Toll-Free 1-888-313-2665

Visit us on the Internet at www.arcadiapublishing.com

*To David L. Dickinson, who generously provided
his rare private collection so that we may enjoy and
preserve our legacy and heritage of the North Country.*

CONTENTS

ACKNOWLEDGMENTS

Stereoscopic Publishers

L.F. Adams, New Bedford, New Hampshire; G.H.Aldrich & Co., Littleton, New Hampshire; American Views, Boston; H.T. Anthony & Co., New York; Clinton H. Atkinson, Penacook, New Hampshire; Bierstadt Bros., New Bedford, Massachusetts; H.P. Bly, Hanover, New Hampshire; Clough & Kimball, Concord, New Hampshire; L. Dowe, Sycamore, Illinois; H.S. Fifield, New Hampton, New Hampshire; J.H. French, Keene, New Hampshire; W.B. Gleason & Son, Whitefield, New Hampshire; C.P. Hibbard, Lisbon, New Hampshire; Kilburn Bros., Littleton, New Hampshire; Little View Co., Littleton, New Hampshire; N.W. Pease, North Conway, New Hampshire; W.M. Pressey, Plymouth, New Hampshire; Frank Rowell, Boston; John P. Soule, Boston; the Treadwell Collection, Joseph Ward, Boston; F. White & Co., Laconia and Lancaster, New Hampshire; and F.J. Young, Campton, New Hampshire.

Special Credits

The Appalachian Mountain Club, John D. Bardwell, F. Allen Bart, Randall H. Bennett, Ronald P. Bergeron, Gladys S. Bickford, Ernest E. Bisbee, the Boston & Maine Railroad, *Chisholm's White Mount Guide*, David Dickinson, *White Mount Echoes*, Benjamin W. English Jr., Francis Ann Johnson Hancock, Robert and Mary Julyan, Richard F. Leavitt, Alexander A. McKenzie, John T.B. Mudge, the Plymouth Historical Society, Edwin B. Robertson, Arthur W. Vose, the Mount Washington Cog Railway Co., and Benjamin G. Willey.

INTRODUCTION

This unique historic publication contains more than 200 rare, reflective stereoscopic photographs of the White Mountains and vicinity via an excursion of the early railroads during the 19th century. The White Mountain region is filled with many wonders, in addition to the unlimited panoramas of the mountains from various vantage points.

The view from the summit of Mount Washington extends for more than 100 miles in all directions and includes within the range of vision 33 other peaks with elevations exceeding 4,000 feet. Whether ascending the Presidential Range by the Carriage Road or the Cog Railway, we will assemble in memory the grandeur and majesty that makes New Hampshire so popular as a four-season resort state. Framing the Presidential Range in the White Mountains are some of the most impressive wonders in the world, namely the Crawford, Franconia, and Pinkham Notches.

Crawford Notch, a New Hampshire State Reservation, has a wonderful scenic ride via the Ogdensburg Railroad along the sides of the mountains. Over high trestles, from Crawford to Fabyan's famous resort hotel, the road in some cases is cut through solid mountain ledges. When we travel by automobile, the scenery is equally grand, the mountains towering above on both sides, dotted with glimmering cascades.

Franconia Notch, another New Hampshire State Reservation, is where the explorer will journey through the Flume, the Pool, the Basin, and view the awesome natural sculpture of the Old Man of the Mountain on Mount Cannon. Pinkham Notch is located on the east side of the Presidential Range, where the Carriage Road begins its ascent up Mount Washington. A brief drive from the base of the mountain takes us to the picturesque Glen Ellis Falls. Points of interest include the Lake of the Clouds on Mount Washington, Echo Lake and Profile Lake in Franconia Notch, and Echo Lake and the White Horse Ledge in North Conway. These places are visited by thousands every year.

The Lakes Region is located just south of the Presidential Range. These magnificent bodies of water abound with beauty. It is easy to assemble a general description of the character of the shore of Winnipesaukee, Squam, Newfound, or Ossipee Lakes; to count its islands; and to enumerate the mountain ranges that surround it. It is not easy to convey with words any impression of the peculiar loveliness that invests it and that lifts them above the rank of a prosaic reservoir in Belknap, Grafton, and Carroll Counties. The lakes, streams, and mountains give an impression of divine art that is renewed each season by its Creator. Poets have written much of this mountainous beauty; however, one poet identified its true impression by writing that "it is the journey, not the arrival, that matters." He surely had the White Mountains in mind.

It would be as easy for an artist to paint the beauty of an autumn sunset as it would be for any writer to describe the natural wonders of the White Mountain scenery; so, in this publication, I will make every attempt at detail and will endeavor to indicate, through this rare collection of stereoscopic views, some of the places that have made these mountains and lakes so special to both natives and visitors alike. *Stereoscopic Views of the White Mountains* has been assembled through the generosity of David L. Dickinson, who has allowed me to format his private collection so all may enjoy these early prints and preserve our legacy of bygone days.

—Bruce D. Heald, Ph.D.

One

MOUNT WASHINGTON: 1860–1890 VIA THE COG RAILWAY

THE SUMMIT OF MOUNT WASHINGTON AND THE COG RAILWAY, C. 1870S. The majestic cone of Mount Washington, crowning the glories of the White Mountain Presidential Range, is the loftiest peak east of the Rocky Mountains and north of the Carolinas, rising to a height of 6,288 feet above sea level. It is written that the climate is the same as Labrador and middle Greenland. The view from the summit sweeps around a circle of nearly 1,000 miles, embracing parts of five states and the province of Quebec. The bold outlines, sides of the crest, and cone of the mountain are broken by narrow ravines that are caught in the dimple of the face of the mountain, in which crystal cascades flow. A railroad, the first of its kind in the world, makes easy access to the summit. On this summit, a house and a restaurant offer all the conveniences for visitors.

THE SUMMIT OF MOUNT WASHINGTON, C. 1870S. Gathered around the Cog Railway trains are summer visitors ready to enjoy an afternoon atop the highest point in the Presidential Range. Nostalgic memories bloom as we reminisce about those days past, when the old Summit House stood majestically on the highest point in New England, Mount Washington. A poet once wrote that it is the journey, not the arrival, that matters; he might well have been writing about New Hampshire's White Mountains.

THE CARRIAGE ROAD, C. 1870S. This road first opened for business on August 8, 1861. Over the first few miles, the road climbs through scenic woods. The gradual ascent provides an excellent conception of the immensity of the mountain and the constantly varied views at turns of the road. The plan to build this road of 8 miles originated with Gen. David O. Macomber, who in 1853 secured a charter for the Mount Washington Turnpike for the Mount Washington Road Company. In the same year, the company was formally organized at the old Alpine House in Gorham, and the general was elected president. Following a survey, construction began in 1855. Two miles of the road was built in the first year.

THE HALFWAY HOUSE ON THE CARRIAGE ROAD. The halfway point (4 miles, 3,840 feet above sea level) is almost exactly at the timberline. From there, the views are spectacular. The 4-mile section of the road to the Ledge above the Halfway House was completed by 1857. Three years later, the road was completed to the summit and was ready for use, operating under the franchise as a turnpike. The credit of the remarkable surveying and engineering achievement belongs to two men—Joseph S. Hall and John P. Rich, contractor and superintendent. A commemorative tablet at Glen records the name and work of John Rich. It is interesting to note that when the road was first opened, users were charged by the mile. If a person was on foot, he was charged 2¢ per mile. A horse and rider cost 3¢ per mile, while a horse and carriage paid 5¢ per mile.

THE HALFWAY HOUSE. At the Halfway House, hardly more than shrubs have been left. The subalpine "buck's horns," the ghostly white trees, are visible as the road continues it ascent up the mountain.

THE GULF OF MEXICO FROM MOUNT WASHINGTON, C. 1880S. Today, this area is known as the "Great Gulf Wilderness." From the Carriage Road, there is an awe-inspiring view into the depths of the Great Gulf, 2 miles in length, 1 mile wide, and 1,500 feet deep of a glacial cirque.

THE LEDGE ON THE MOUNT WASHINGTON CARRIAGE ROAD, LOOKING UP THE MOUNTAIN, C. 1880S. Doubling and redoubling on itself, the road reaches the the rocky eminence known as Ledge, where there is an awe-inspiring view into the depths of the Great Gulf.

THE MOUNT
WASHINGTON CARRIAGE
ROAD BELOW THE
LEDGE, C. 1880S. For
hundreds of years, Mount
Washington (named
in 1784) has been the
goal of adventurous
visitors from every state.
With the building of
the Carriage Road in
1861, ascent has become
effortless, and traffic is
now continuous in
fair weather.

THE LIZZIE BOURNE
MONUMENT ON MOUNT
WASHINGTON. This cairn
is one of the many that
mark the trails along the
Appalachian Mountain
Range from Georgia to
Maine for the thousands of
hikers who make
the venture.

13

THE SUMMIT HOUSE FROM THE CARRIAGE ROAD, C. 1870S. The Mount Washington Carriage Road was the world's first mountain toll road and the scene of many races and endurance tests. P.T. Barnum called the view from the top of the mountain "the second greatest show on earth." The Native Americans thought the Great Spirit lived on the summit of the highest peak in the Northeast. From this vantage point, the view unfolds on every side: in the south lie New Hampshire's Lakes Region, river valleys, and the Berkshires of Massachusetts; in the west lie Vermont's Green Mountains and New York's Adirondacks; and to the north is Canada. To the east is Maine; along its broken coastline stretches the Atlantic Ocean, from which this mountaintop was first seen by navigators hundreds of years ago.

THE ARRIVAL OF GUESTS AND CARRIAGES ON THE SUMMIT OF MOUNT WASHINGTON, C. 1875. Many visitors to the summit enjoyed ascending the mountain by horse and buggy so they might travel via the Carriage Road on the east side of the mountain.

14

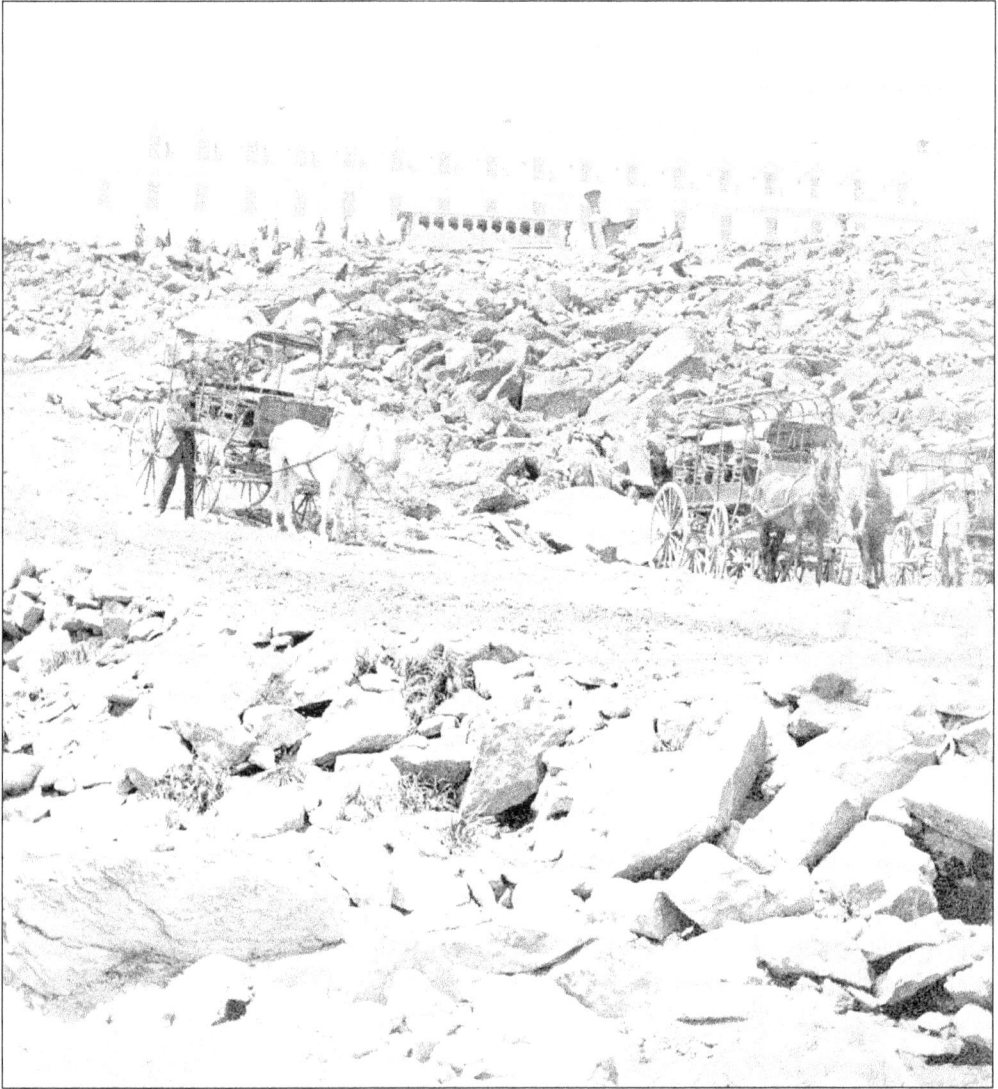

THE MOUNT WASHINGTON SUMMIT HOUSE FROM THE CARRIAGE ROAD, C. 1870S. This majestic cone is the crowning glory of the White Mountain Presidential Range. Its boldness of granite rocks pile ever upward into the clouds. The first shelter for visitors to the summit was built of stone in 1821. The original Summit House, built in July 1852, was demolished in 1884 to make room for a modern Summit House. In 1908, the second house was destroyed by fire; it was soon replaced in 1915 by a new two-story Summit House that featured an entrance directly from the Mount Washington Cog Railway station platform.

A SELECT EXCURSION PARTY ON THE PIAZZA OF THE MOUNT WASHINGTON SUMMIT HOUSE, JULY 1877. Thousands of seasonal tourists came to parade the spacious platform and enjoy the spectacle of beauty atop New England. Here, we see them waiting for the arrival of the railway train to take them down the mountain.

THE MOUNT WASHINGTON SUMMIT HOUSE DINING ROOM, c. 1870s. A major feature of this fine old house was the dining room that could accommodate more than 80 guests. Included also was a lounging room with a spacious fireplace, a waiting room, and a souvenir stand—all on the first floor. Eighteen rooms and the lavatories were on the second floor.

THE MOUNT WASHINGTON DEPOT-OBSERVATORY, DURING THE WINTER OF 1870–1871. Sergeants Smith and Nelson are shown prospecting.

THE FROST AT WORK CLOSE-UP ON MOUNT WASHINGTON, SEPTEMBER 4, 1872. The winters in the White Mountains are long and cold. The land is rocky, and life is hard. The everlasting hills brood over men who live in their shadows, and men who know the mountains love them.

THE INTERIOR OF THE MOUNT WASHINGTON SUMMIT HOUSE. Shown is a rare photograph taken on February 11, 1862, illustrating one of the rooms before the house was demolished in 1884.

THE INTERIOR OF THE MOUNT WASHINGTON SUMMIT HOUSE, C. 1862. This stereoscopic picture is entitled *Frost at Work*. It shows the thickness of the ice on open beams.

The Mount Washington Summit House after a Frost, c. 1860s. Two visitors are shown taking one last view of the Presidential Range from atop Mount Washington before winter takes command of the mountain.

The U.S. Observatory. In 1869, C.H. Hitchcock, a professor of geology at Dartmouth College, and his assistant, J.H. Huntington, were granted permission to adapt the engine house of the Cog Railway for use as an observatory.

THE INTERIOR OF THE U.S. OBSERVATORY AND SIGNAL STATION. On November 13, 1870, a five-man crew, including an observer and telegrapher for the U.S. Signal Service (which at the time, made weather observations), began regular observations. The program continued year-round until 1887. Afterward, the station was manned only in the summer until 1892. From 1874, the observers were housed in the so-called Signal Station, which remained on the summit until the great fire of 1908.

THE INTERIOR OF THE U.S. OBSERVATORY ON MOUNT WASHINGTON. Before another long and busy day on the summit, these three gentlemen take advantage of a relaxing moment and good conversation after a late breakfast.

20

WINTER AT THE TIP TOP HOUSE, 1870–1871. The frost here is 2 feet thick.

WINTER AT THE TIP TOP HOUSE. Winters are extremely harsh on the summit. The lowest temperature ever recorded on the summit is –46 degrees Fahrenheit. The highest wind velocity ever recorded was set at 231 mph during a gust measured on April 12, 1934. The staff members who recorded those high winds were Wendell Stephenson, Alexander McKenzie, and Salvatore Pagliuca.

21

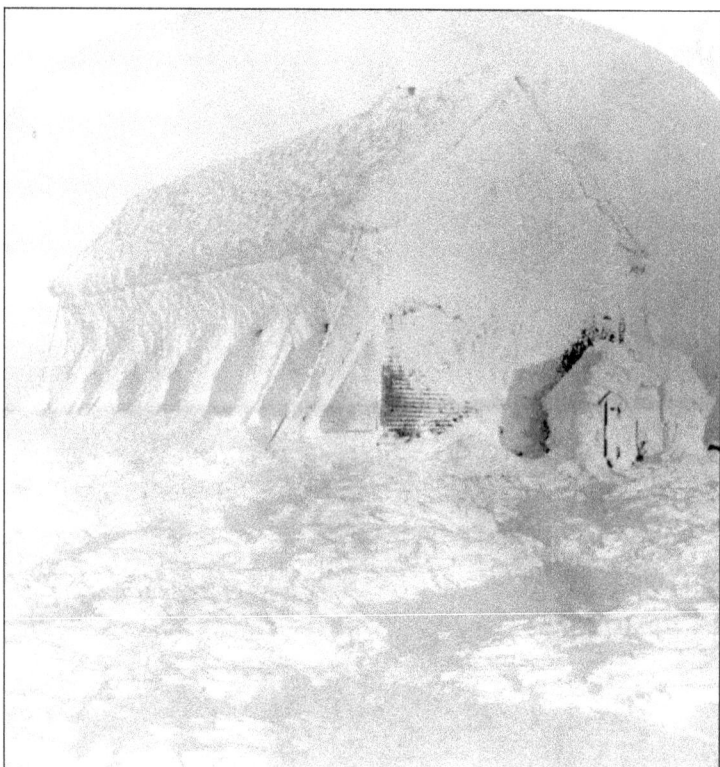

ANOTHER VIEW OF WINTER AT THE TIP TOP HOUSE, 1870–1871. During the winter, it was almost impossible to navigate about the summit.

A CARRIAGE IN FRONT OF THE TIP TOP HOUSE ON MOUNT WASHINGTON, c. 1875. The road continues at an increasing altitude until it approaches the cogwheel railroad. The road then curves around the rocky plateau to the summit, on which the most conspicuous structure is the low, wooden, solidly built Summit House.

THE TIP TOP HOUSE,
c. 1870s. This house
was constructed in July
1853. Like the first
Summit House, it had
granite walls several feet
thick. This house was
28 feet wide and 84 feet
long. It had a deck roof,
on which a visitor could
stand and look down
6,288 feet to the vast
map spread out on every
side at his feet.

THE TIP TOP HOUSE,
c. 1870s. This house
was later renovated
to make it a more
suitable shelter for
visitors. Originally,
cables anchored in
the mountain kept
the building from
blowing away during
high winds. Cement
and iron rods held it
in proud defiance of
wind and storm to
the bleakest crag of
Mount Washington.

23

THE INTERIOR OF THE TIP TOP HOUSE, c. 1870s. The only newspaper printed on the summit of any mountain in the world was published here under the title *Among the Clouds*. Established in 1877, it was the oldest summer resort newspaper in America. Publication of the paper ceased in 1915, when the Tip Top House was destroyed by fire.

THE TIP TOP HOUSE WITH VISITORS ON THE SUMMIT OF MOUNT WASHINGTON, c. 1870s. From 1884 until 1908, this house was used for a variety of purposes, including tourist accommodations and a restaurant. In 1908, after surviving the conflagration that destroyed all other buildings at the summit, it again became the only available accommodation for guests; it served as such until August 29, 1915, when the Summit House restaurant was completed.

SEASONAL TOURISTS AT THE TIP TOP HOUSE, C. 1870s. This moment of pleasantry allows new visitors to the summit as they absorb the never-ending view to the horizon miles away—north to Canada, east to the Atlantic Ocean, south to Lake Winnipesaukee, and west to Vermont.

THE SUMMIT OF MOUNT WASHINGTON, C. 1870s. To the left is the Tip Top House. The Cog Railroad train is to the right.

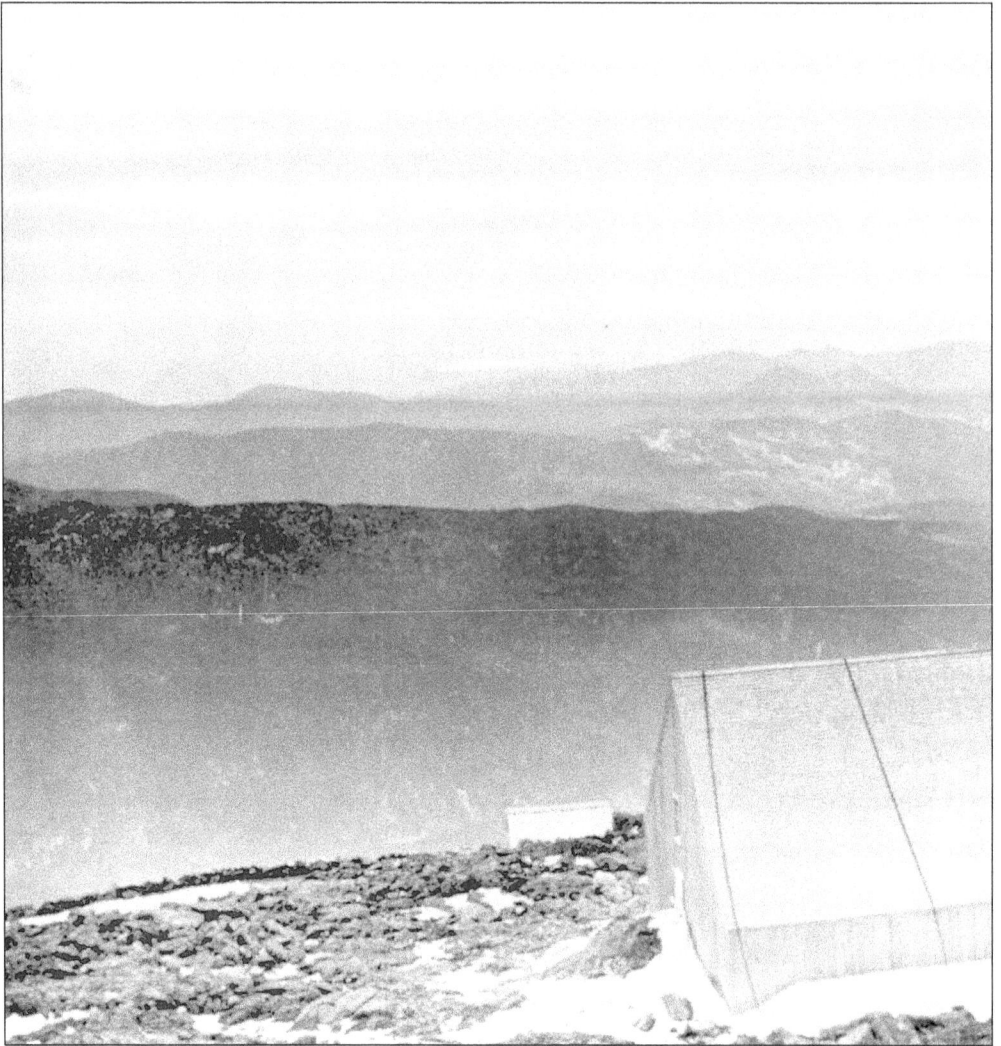

A VIEW FROM MOUNT WASHINGTON LOOKING EAST, C. 1880S. The view from the summit of Mount Washington is much the same as it appeared to the early settlers—the changless cliffs and crags, the rock-strewn riverbeds, and the forested mountain slopes. This beautiful land, where highways follow the rivers through the notches, is a place of scenic grandeur and a great playground where tens of thousands spend vacations or weekends.

THE OLD PEPPERSASS, JULY 20, 1929. Shown is the old *Peppersass* proudly posing for its railroad friends. After its fatal crash into Burt Ravine in 1929, various parts were salvaged, reassembled, and placed on exhibition at the Base Station. This engine was the first ever built for the Cog Railway. It was so named because of its resemblance to a pepper sauce bottle. *Peppersass* served well until 1878, when it was retired. Engines with horizontal boilers took the places of *Peppersass* and *Stephenson*. In 1928, *Peppersass* was brought out of retirement by the Baltimore & Ohio Railroad to appear at the Fair of the Iron Horse in Halethorpe, Maryland. On July 20, 1929, there was a gala festival, including a final run up the mountain. However, something went wrong; just before it reached a section of track known as Jacob's Ladder, the old engine went down the mountain, around a curve at a terrific speed, and onto the rocks in Burt Ravine. Since that time, there have been no more experiments with relics of the past.

THE COG RAILWAY UP MOUNT WASHINGTON, c. 1870s. The invention of the Cog Railway came from Herrick Aiken of Franklin, New Hampshire. But it was Sylvester Marsh who pushed the project through to completion. In the summer of 1866, a quarter-mile section of the track was built, including a trestle bridge crossing the Ammonoosuc River. On August 29, 1866, the first practical demonstration of the Cog Railway was held. The engine took its load of 40 passengers up a grade of 15 degrees quite easily.

THE RAILROAD UP MOUNT WASHINGTON, c. 1870s. The essential feature of the Cog Railway is the driving mechanism. On the track, in addition to the outside rails, there is a central cog rail consisting of two pieces of wrought-angle iron, placed parallel and connected by iron pins 4 inches apart. Teeth on the driving wheel of the engine mesh with the cog rail and draw the whole train up the mountain.

JACOB'S LADDER, MOUNT
WASHINGTON RAILWAY,
c. 1870s. This massive trestle,
over which the cogwheel
engine pushes the coach 3
miles up the steep side of
Mount Washington, has an
average grade of 1,300 feet
and a maximum grade of 1,980
feet to the mile. At this point,
the tree line ends and the
subalpine vegetation begins.
There is no doubt that one
of the greatest impressions of
the ride from the Base Station
to the summit of Mount
Washington is the crossing of
Jacob's Ladder.

THE COG RAILWAY
TRAINS CROSSING JACOB'S
LADDER, c. 1870s. The
air grows colder as we
ascend the mountain.
Here, there is a view of
the southern peaks of the
Presidential Range. A
little farther up, the train
climbs the Long Trestle.
The peaks of Mounts Clay
and Jefferson rise to the
left. Close at hand is the
almost sheer drop of more
than 1,000 feet into
Burt Ravine.

THE ASCENT OF MOUNT WASHINGTON VIA THE COG RAILWAY, c. 1870s. Daily, the wood-burning engine with early-type vertical boiler is loaded with passengers eager to arrive at the top of New England.

THE COG RAILWAY ON THE SUMMIT OF MOUNT WASHINGTON, c. 1870s. Visitors disembark from the train in this 19th-century photograph.

A VIEW FROM THE SUMMIT OF MOUNT WASHINGTON WITH THE COG RAILWAY IN THE FOREGROUND, C. 1870S. The Presidential Range can be seen in the distance.

THE RAILWAY UP MOUNT WASHINGTON, C. 1870S. This close view shows the old steam engine used for the first cog railway up the mountain.

SLIDING DOWN THE MOUNT WASHINGTON RAILWAY. This may look like sport, but to right-of-way maintenance men, it was simply a quick way to beat the five o'clock whistle to the Base Station after a day's work on the mountain. About 3 feet long and 1 foot wide, the slide board was made of wood and was reinforced with metal. It fitted over the cog rail and had two friction-brake handles, one on either side. These were equipped with pieces of metal that slid under the projecting side flanges of the cog rail. By pulling up on these handles, the speed of the slide board could be checked. No one but workers were ever permitted to use them, as it required both experience and strength to manage a slide board safely. This track inspector on the Cog Railway was photographed in 1929.

THREE MEN SLIDING DOWN THE RAILWAY, C. 1890S. These slide boards were born out of necessity. There was no other way for track workers to get home to the base boardinghouse at the end of the working day on the mountain. They were used up to about 1930 when, because of a few fatal accidents, their use was banned. No mechanical error was found to have contributed to the accidents. A popular nickname for the slide board was the "Devil's Shingle."

SLIDING DOWN JACOB'S
LADDER, C. 1890S.
A typical time for
the 3-mile slide was
approximately 10
minutes. Two minutes
and 45 seconds was
the record.

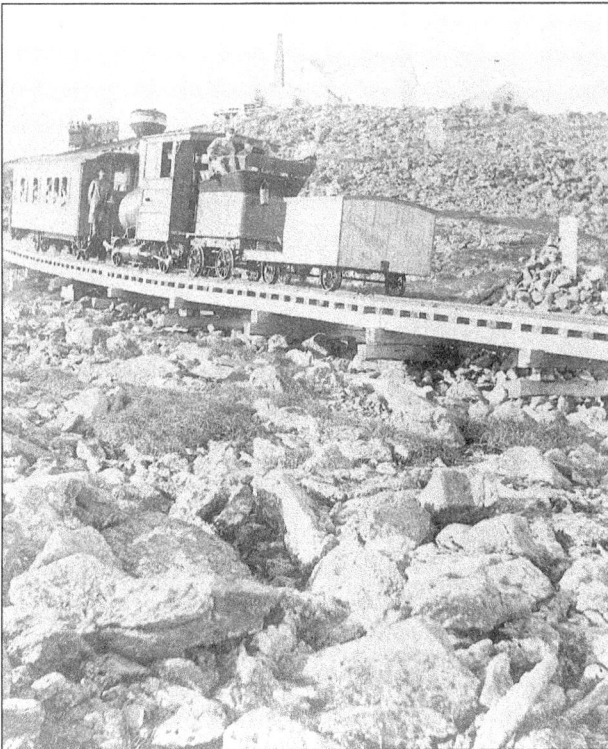

THE COG RAILROAD ASCENDING
THE MOUNTAIN,
c. 1890S. Chisholm's guide book
describes the Cog as follows:
"The locomotives are queer
looking pieces of machinery,
chunky and ungainly but of
enormous power." In ascending
Mount Washington, the engine
pushes the passenger car, which
is never coupled to the engine
during the trip. After the first
quarter mile, the trip is entirely
built on a trestle ranging from 2
feet to 30 feet off the ground.

THE COG RAILWAY TRAINS AT THE SUMMIT HOUSE OF MOUNT WASHINGTON, C. 1880s. In the distance to the left are the many visitors taking their last panoramic view from the summit before boarding the train for the descent of the mountain.

THE MOUNT WASHINGTON RAILWAY TRESTLE, LOOKING DOWN THE MOUNTAIN, C. 1870s. Some hikers walk the trestle.

34

THE RAILWAY ON MOUNT WASHINGTON, LOOKING DOWN TO THE BASE STATION, C. 1870S. When the Mount Washington Railroad opened, its greatest handicap was its location in the middle dense woods, 25 miles from the nearest railroad station in Littleton and 12 miles from the nearest hotel. The only approach was over the turnpike from Fabyan, which was constructed in 1866. This image shows the sawmill and the first repair shop at the Base Station.

THE RAILWAY BASE STATION. In 1876, the Boston, Concord, & Montreal Railroad (BC & M) extended its tracks to a new terminal at the Base Station, about a half mile below Marshfield. The Cog Railway was then built downward to connect with the feeder line. On the trip from Fabyan, the passengers rode in an open-air car pushed by the engine, so that they could enjoy the view, minus the dust and smoke.

THE RAILWAY BASE STATION. In 1858, Sylvester Marsh exhibited a model of his engine and cog railway to the New Hampshire state legislature; he was granted a charter to build a steam railway up Mount Washington and Lafayette, although few thought it would ever work. His first job was to build a turnpike to the location now known as the base station, some distance below where passengers now take the train. The terminal is now at Marshfield, a coined place name commemoration Marsh and Darby Field.

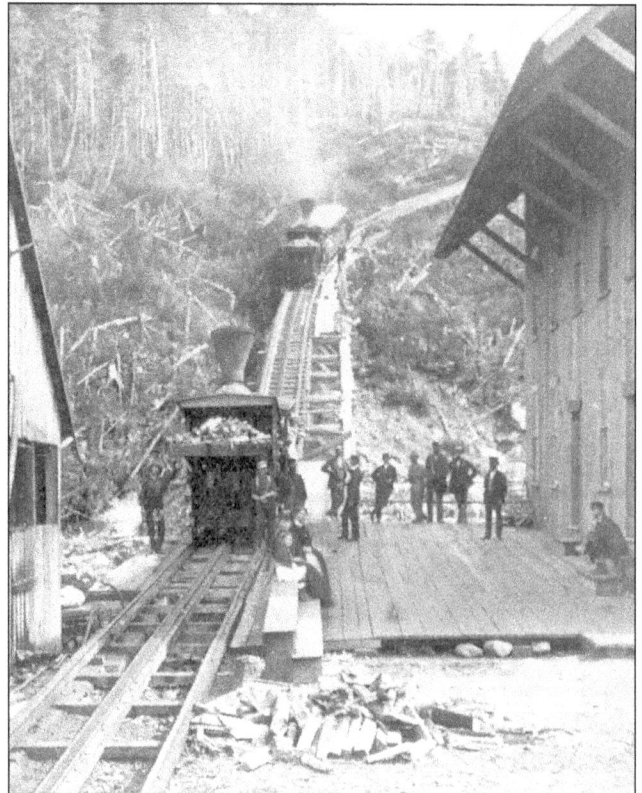

THE MOUNT WASHINGTON BASE STATION. It is from here that the curious little inclined trains start on their way to the summit of Mount Washington. Sylvester Marsh of Littleton, New Hampshire, was the first to have the idea to build a mountain-climbing railroad.

THE MOUNT WASHINGTON BASE STATION WITH CONCORD STAGECOACHES AND PASSENGERS FROM THE CRAWFORD HOUSE AND OTHER HOTELS, c. 1875. Thousands of visitors have come to ride the railway to the summit. It is interesting to note that the first president of the United States to visit Mount Washington during his term of office was Ulysses S. Grant. On August 27, 1869, he and Mrs. Grant with their son, Jesse, drove from the Crawford House to Marshfield. He was welcomed by Sylvester Marsh, whom he complimented on his enterprise. At the summit, he was greeted by Col. J.R. Hitchcock, landlord of the Tip Top House, where the party dined and was entertained. On August 20, 1877, Pres. Rutherford B. Hayes and family made the ascent via the Cog Railway.

THE MOUNT WASHINGTON GULF STATION, c. 1880s.

TWO COG RAILWAY TRAINS ASCENDING MOUNT WASHINGTON, C. 1880S. In the summer of 1866, construction was pushed, and a quarter-mile section of track was built. On August 28 that year, a newspaper correspondent wrote, "The stockholders and parties in interest of the Mount Washington Steam Railway Company are to assemble tomorrow in the Notch of the White Mountains, near the old Fabyan stand, to witness a trial trip on the first and lower section of this remarkable work." The next day, the public demonstration was held, and the reporter commented, "The engine works to a charm, taking its load of 40 passengers up a grade of 15 degrees with the utmost care."

TWO WORKMEN TAKING SUPPLIES UP MOUNT WASHINGTON VIA THE COG RAILWAY, C. 1880S. Two maintenance men are shown transporting supplies and making a daily inspection of the railway—safety is a priority.

THE THOUSAND STREAMS ABOVE THE SNOW ARCH IN TUCKERMAN RAVINE, MOUNT WASHINGTON. Tuckerman Ravine may well be called a "mountain colosseum." It is about a mile in length, one-half mile wide, and 1,000 feet deep. It is one of the great glacial cirques. These cirques were almost entirely scooped out by glacial action. Although not so deep as some of the other ravines, the steepness and sweep of its surrounding cliffs make it impressive. Its back wall is called the "Fall of a Thousand Streams," since countless rivulets drip down its almost perpendicular sides. It is possible that the glistening of these rivulets in the sunlight may have given rise to the early tradition of a Great Carbuncle here.

UNDER THE SNOW ARCH IN TUCKERMAN RAVINE, C. 1880S. This arch is one of the most striking spectacles in the White Mountains. Not always in arch formation, this phenomenon is formed by deposits of snow blown over the edge of the rocky plateau that creates the eastern wall of the ravine.

THE SNOW ARCH IN TUCKERMAN RAVINE, c. 1880s. An incipient glacier is formed at the bottom where accumulations of snow are piled through the winter to a depth of 200 or 300 feet. During many summers, the sun is unable to melt the snow down to this underlying interior part. Rivulets from the head wall, uniting farther down in the Ellis River, frequently wear an arch in the snow, which gives the formation its common name. Varying in size, it has reached dimensions of 255 feet in length, 84 feet in width, and an arch 40 feet high.

THE LAKE OF THE CLOUDS, c. 1870s. This small alpine pool serves as the source of the Ammonoosuc River. It is located a short distance from the summit of Mount Washington in a small bowl on the northwest side of the ridge, near the low point between Mount Washington and Mount Monroe. There are two lakes; the larger of them, often called the Lower Lake, is at an elevation of 5,025 with an area of 1.2 acres, while the much smaller Upper Lake has an elevation of 5,050 feet, with an area of .4 acres.

Two

THE CRAWFORD NOTCH
AND THE GREAT CUT

THE PASS OF THE CRAWFORD NOTCH VIA FRANKENSTEIN TRESTLE, C. 1870S. Here we see the Portland and Ogdensburg Railroad on a scheduled trip over the Frankenstein Trestle in the Crawford Notch. The clearing in the distance ends abruptly as the tracks and highway climb again into the deep forest for another 3 miles, rising nearly 700 feet as it ascends from 1,320 feet at the clearing to 1,989 feet at Saco Lake. High above the stony stream and opposite the railroad that snakes around steep slopes, the opening twists between the towering sides of Mount Willey (4,216 feet) and the bald ledges of Mount Willard (2,786), on the left, and Mount Webster (3,876) and Mount Jackson (4,012), on the right. On its way, it passes the Silver and Flume Cascades, each a series of leaping waterfalls that drop more than 1,100 feet.

41

THE PORTLAND & OGDENSBURG (P & O) RAILROAD ON THE FRANKENSTEIN TRESTLE WITH MOUNT WEBSTER IN THE BACKGROUND, C. 1870s. This spectacular side view shows the Portland and Ogdensburg Railroad as it travels on its scheduled service trip to the Fabyan House, on the north side of Crawford Notch in August 1875.

FRANKENSTEIN TRESTLE AND TRAIN, P & O RAILROAD, CRAWFORD NOTCH, NEW HAMPSHIRE, C. 1875. The steam railroad crosses the trestle with Crawford Notch in the background. The successor to the stagecoach was the steam railroad; New Hampshire pioneered in the use of steam for transportation. Following Morey's steamboat, the first steam fire engine was built by Nehemiah Bean in Gilmanton, New Hampshire. Later, the Amoskeag fire engines would be widely known. The coming of the railroad took place in the first half of the 19th century; the first New Hampshire railroad was the Nashua & Lowell, chartered in 1835 and operational between the two cities in 1838. Gradually, the Boston & Maine Railroad secured a monopoly. By 1901, the Boston and Maine dominated the railroad mileage in the state.

FRANKENSTEIN TRESTLE AND P & O RAILROAD, SIDE VIEW, C. 1875. As the railway approaches Crawford Notch ahead, the vigilant travelers, looking forward on the right, will get one of the grandest views of Mount Washington; this prospect has long been famed for its sublimity. Presently, the deep Frankenstein Gulf is crossed on the trestles of iron, 500 feet long and 80 feet high. After crossing the trestle, there is nothing but a shelf cut by the indomitable will of man from the mountainside, for the passage of the train that ever increases in altitude until the summit of the divide is reached.

FRANKENSTEIN CLIFF, P & O RAILROAD, c. 1870s. Five hundred feet above the Saco Valley, the train climbs the mountainside. Bordering the chasm on either side are lofty mountains surrounding this vantage point in the heart of Crawford Notch. In front, the precipitous cliff appear to bar further progress, while farther up the notch, majestically grand at the head of a succession of peaks, appears Mount Washington, "the Crown Jewel of New England."

THE DANGER SIGNAL, THE RAILROAD OF LIFE, c. 1870s. Inspection and safety of the tracks and trestle was a major concern for the P & O Railroad. It was here that many open observation cars halted briefly so passengers could witness the vista about them. This much-photographed location was (and still is) considered by many visitors as "the Heart of the Notch."

THE P & O RAILROAD TRAIN IN CRAWFORD NOTCH DURING THE WINTER, c. 1870s. Keeping the railroad open through the notch during the winter months was always a challenge. The extreme temperature changes and snowfall were quite hazardous throughout mountain railroading. In a very short span of time, high winds often prevail in the notch, creating snowdrifts several feet deep.

MOUNT WEBSTER FROM THE
CRAWFORD HOUSE, C. 1870S.
One of the finest views in the
notch is where the bases of
Mounts Willard, Webster, and
Willey approach each other. The
descent through the notch is said
to give a more marked impression
of its grandeur than the ascent.

THE CRAWFORD HOUSE FROM THE
ELEPHANT'S HEAD,
C. 1870S. In the far distance is
the imposing view of the grand
old hotel, the Crawford House.
The first Crawford House was
constructed in 1852, on a knoll
west of Saco Lake to meet the
accommodating needs of the
wealthy tourists from the city.

SACO LAKE AND THE CRAWFORD HOUSE, c. 1880s. The original hotel with that name was started in 1852 by Thomas J. Crawford, a brother of Ethan Allen Crawford. Having run into financial difficulties, he sold the unfinished buildings to J.L. Gibb, who completed the hotel. In 1854, the original building was burned, but a new and larger hotel was constructed in 1859. That building is the nucleus of the present hostelry. A sign near Crawford House marks the site of an early hotel, the Notch House, built by Abel Crawford and son Ethan Allen in 1828, and kept by another son, Thomas J., from 1829 to 1853, when it was burned.

THE CRAWFORD HOUSE WITH A PARTY OF GUESTS PREPARING TO GO UP MOUNT WASHINGTON, c. 1880s. In this old inn, naturalist Henry Thoreau, historian Francis Parkman, and "Prose Poet" Starr King vacationed.

A View from the Crawford House, Looking South to the Notch, c. 1870s. Before its discovery in 1771, the Crawford Notch was an unexplored expanse of mountain wilderness. The area was known only to the Native Americans, but even local tribes seldom entered its shadows because of the superstitious awe of the high mountains framing the pass. Only war parties of Canadian Indians, bringing captives home from the New England coastal settlements, ventured through the notch way.

The Gates of the Crawford Notch, c. 1880s. No one realized there was a notch wide enough for a good road to connect the coastal villages and inland settlements until Lancaster pioneer Timothy Nash, in 1771, accidentally saw it from a high vantage point (a tree) during a hunting trip. He quickly made his way down toward the narrow opening between gray cliffs at the base of steep mountain walls to announce his discovery to others.

47

THE CRAWFORD NOTCH ROAD AFTER A STORM, C. 1870s. It was not long after finding the byway in the notch that two men chopped underbrush, filled in holes, rolled rocks aside, and heaved branches out of the way so that a narrow way was cleared and they could continue their 90-mile trek south to Portsmouth, New Hampshire. The proposed notch road was first laid out as hardly more than a rough trail.

CRAWFORD NOTCH, NEW HAMPSHIRE, C. 1870s. The notch was named for the Abel Crawford family, who guided tourists through the scenic grandeur of the White Hills. The Crawfords operated the first inn in this region, cut the first trail to the summit of Mount Washington, and pioneered in opening the White Mountains to the public. The tenth New Hampshire turnpike twisted through the notch northward to connect Coos County with the seacoast, where local products such as potash, pelts, and assorted dairy products were exchanged for loads of merchandise from Portland, Portsmouth, and other points south.

48

THE NOTCH, NEW HAMPSHIRE, C. 1870S. The old view of "the Gateway" prior to the building of the railroad illustrates the rough terrain through which the first P & O Railroad planned to build. The Saco River, located a few hundred feet beyond the Gateway, flows through the narrow cut along with the tenth New Hampshire turnpike.

THE GATES OF THE NOTCH AND THE GREAT CUT, P & O RAILROAD, CRAWFORD NOTCH, 1875. The proposed notch road was first laid out as hardly more than a rough trail.

49

THE GREAT CUT, THE P & O RAILROAD, CRAWFORD NOTCH, 1875. The rocks and boulders from the Great Cut were hauled away on a temporary track and placed into the marshland as fill for the railway. Building the railroad through Crawford Notch was an extremely difficult feat. In fact, most engineers said it could not be done. However, two men took the challenge. Gen. Samuel J. Anderson of Portland, Maine, and John F. Anderson of South Windham, Maine, made it happen. They strung bridges across gorges that no one could have spanned.

THE P & O RAILROAD PASS, CRAWFORD NOTCH, NEW HAMPSHIRE, 1875. Nearing completion, the tracks are carefully placed near the turn of the notch. The plan of the rail route was to connect Portland, Maine, with northern Vermont and Canada, including the shortcut through the gap in the White Mountains.

THE CRAWFORD HOUSE (FROM THE P & O RAILROAD), CRAWFORD NOTCH PASS, 1875. The men of the P & O Railroad used hand tools, push cars, and muscle in cutting the Gateway through the notch.

THE PASS THROUGH CRAWFORD NOTCH, P & O RAILROAD, C. 1870S. One of the grandest views in the East is found in this notch. Here, the walls of rock mount higher and higher and press closer and closer together, until they crowd the scant doorway through which man has made an entrance for both himself and the iron horse. From the narrow defile, the mountains on either side sweep away, falling into the watershed of the Saco River on the one hand and the Connecticut River on the other. Here is the ganglion of travel through the White Mountains and the mightiest of all the mountain scenes.

THE P & O RAILROAD PASS, CRAWFORD NOTCH, NEW HAMPSHIRE, 1875. Beside the railway is the roadway in the narrows of the pass, which in time became one of the most active tourist highways in the North Country.

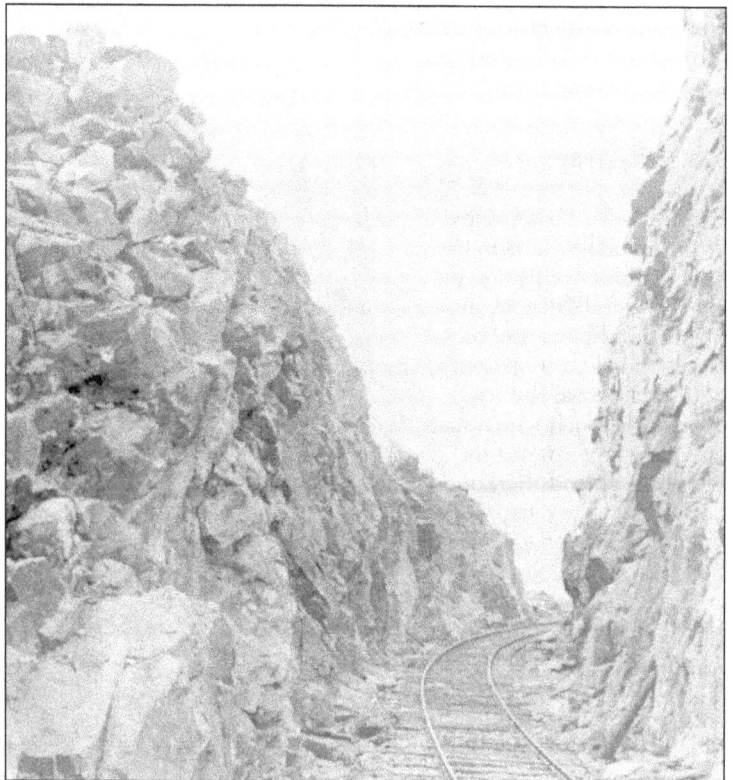

THE P & O RAILROAD PASS, CRAWFORD NOTCH, NEW HAMPSHIRE, 1875. Great pains were taken to create proper footing for the tracks. Thus, the P & O workers had to blast through ledges along the base of Mount Willard. For nine consecutive miles, the grade was 116 feet to each mile.

THE LOCOMOTIVE THE MOUNTAINER IN THE CRAWFORD NOTCH PASS, C. LATE 1870s. The ride of 27 miles from North Conway to the Crawford House took approximately one and a half hours. According the early town reports, the first produce carried over this road was a barrel of rum from Portland to Lancaster, a gift to anyone who could get it through the notch. Captain Rosebrook accomplished the feat, although nearly all of the contents were consumed en route by "those who helped manage the affair."

THE GREAT CUT AND A P & O TRAIN, CRAWFORD NOTCH PASS, 1875. The Portland & Ogdensburg Railroad Company was chartered in Maine in February 1867 and in New Hampshire in 1869. Although the intention to reach Ogdensburg never materialized in four and a half years, the line extended from Portland to North Conway, and in August 1875, it was opened to "Giant Grave" at Fabyan, where the Crawfords and Rosebrooks had arrived in the late 1700s as pioneers. A popular guidebook announced, "No other railroad in the region traverses such imposing scenery, wild gorges [and] majestic peaks." The book advised passengers to sit on the right side of the train for the finest views during the northward ride.

"A Moment of Reflection—Success," the Great Gorge, Crawford Notch, 1875. A memorial bronze plaque, honoring the builders of the Portland and Ogdensburg Railroad, was placed in a shady nook beside Route 302. The inscription reads as follows:

In Memoriam
Samuel Jamieson Anderson, John Farwell Anderson
1824–1905, 1823–1887
President Chief Engineer
on the Portland & Ogdensburg Railroad, the organization and construction of which was due to their untiring energy and skill.
John Anderson
1853–1911
Son of Samuel Jamieson Anderson, through his life a lover of these mountains and active in the development of this region.

THE ELEPHANT'S HEAD
(UPPER LEFT) AND THE
GATEWAY TO CRAWFORD
NOTCH FROM THE
CRAWFORD HOUSE,
c. 1860. Just beyond the
site of the old Crawford
House, towering 100 feet
above the Carriage Road, is
a huge boulder, shaped like
the head of an elephant,
the trunk of which reaches
to the roadway. A few yards
to the right, the railroad
emerges through the Great
Cut in the mountainside.

THE FABYAN HOUSE AND THE P & O RAILROAD, c. 1880s. The Fabyan House, named in honor of the well-known innkeeper Horace Fabyan, opened to guests in 1873. Shortly thereafter, it became one of most fashionable resorts in the White Mountains. Centrally located, this hotel and station soon became the most important railroad point in the mountain region. This site is of interest because of its connection with a mound known as the "Giant's Grave," which was here when Eleazer Rosebrook came as a settler in 1792. Before this hotel was erected, the mound was leveled, which apparently removed the curse from the spot. Near its base, Ethan Allen Crawford, Rosebrook's grandson, built an inn that was burned to the ground in 1803, as did the two others after it. By tradition, the place was haunted by a Native American spirit that declared, "No pale-face shall take root here; this the Great Spirit whispered in my ear." All Boston and New York express trains ran to and from this station, as did the Mount Washington trains, via the Crawford Notch.

THE BOSTON & MAINE, NO. 494, C. 1900S. At the turn of the 19th century, the Boston & Maine dominated the rail service through New Hampshire and much of the Northeast. Today, we find many of these old steam iron horses sitting idle on exhibit in the remote railroad yard or near the roundhouse in North Conway, New Hampshire.

STRATTON & COMPANY NO. 3, C. 1900S. A century ago, it would be commonplace to see this train pass through the notch on a pleasant Sunday afternoon, loaded with visitors from the city.

ANOTHER VIEW OF THE STRATTON & COMPANY NO. 3, C. 1900S. During the winter months, the train service in the White Mountains became more difficult; however, rail service got through regardless of the weather.

Three

THE FRANCONIA NOTCH
AND THE FLUME

THE OLD MAN OF THE MOUNTAIN, C. 1870S. This granite formation is considered the most perfect, natural stone face in the world. This picture is taken from an 1878 stereopticon view by the Kilburn brothers of Littleton, New Hampshire. Also called the "Profile," the "Great Stone Face" of Hawthorne's story consists of five ledges that give it the appearance of a human face. This profile, which is 40 feet in height, is located on the south end of Cannon Mountain, 1,400 feet above the ever beautiful Profile Lake. It is recorded that the Old Man of the Mountain was first seen in 1805 by Francis Whitcomb and Luke Brooks, two workmen who were working on the notch road.

THE OLD MAN OF THE MOUNTAIN PROFILE AMONG THE CLOUDS, c. 1870s. The craggy countenance is one never to be tired of, as it seems to play, under varying conditions, with almost human moods. The expression is noble, and those who can see it with a thundercloud behind it will carry away the grandest impression. This profile is unquestionably the most remarkable natural curiosity in this country, if not the world.

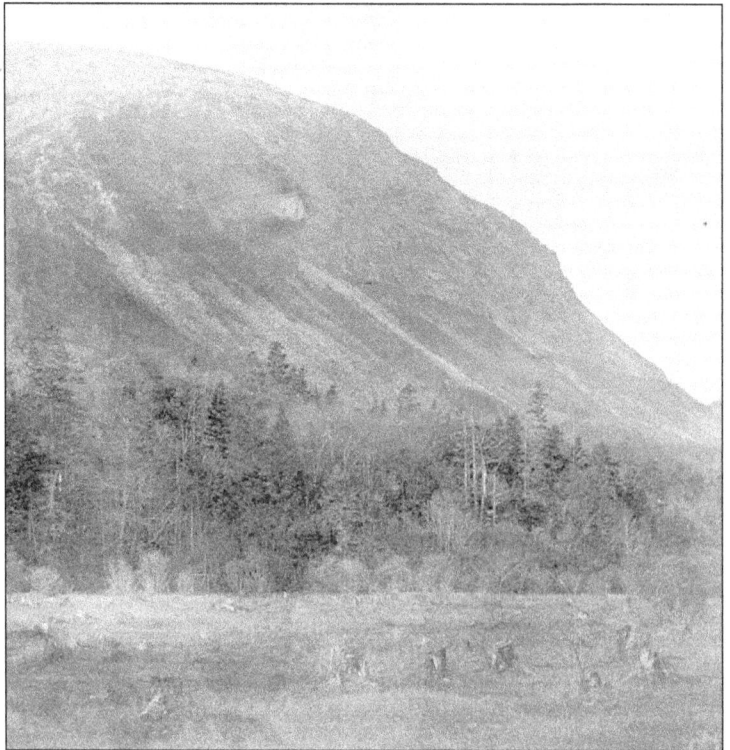

CANNON MOUNTAIN, c. 1880s. The origin of this mountain's name is derived from the oblong rock near the summit that has the appearance of a cannon. Upon a closer examination, you may notice that there are knobs on Kinsman Ridge, south of Cannon Mountain; they are called the cannon balls. The profile of the Old Man of the Mountain is located on the east ridge of this mountain.

PROFILE LAKE, FRANCONIA NOTCH, 1875. This beautiful mountain lake is located at the foot of Cannon Mountain and nearly surrounded by virgin forest. It was formerly called Ferrin's Pond and then the Old Man's Washbowl. South, 500 feet along a brookside path from the parking lot, is a fine vantage point on the edge of Profile Lake, where a boulder marker has been placed by the state. About four o'clock is the best time to view the gigantic silhouette of the Old Man of the Mountain against the blue sky. It was not uncommon to see the young ladies in their summer finery grace the shoreline of the lake for an afternoon picnic.

PROFILE LAKE WITH VACATIONERS, c. 1870s. For a romantic moment on the lake, boating was very popular and often seen on a quiet Sunday afternoon. Located at the base of the Old Man's profile, at the gateway to Franconia Notch in the White Mountains, the lake reflects the peace and tranquillity of days past. Yet the purple hues of the rockface and the somber greens of the forest on the mountainsides relieve the sternness of the hills that frame the lake and soften the sublimity with grace.

THE PROFILE HOUSE, FRANCONIA NOTCH DURING THE WINTER, c. 1870s. Located near the Old Man of the Mountain, the Profile House became a very popular summer resort for the rich and famous tourists. The first house opened in 1853; it burned, was rebuilt, and burned again. The third Profile House was built by Col. Charles Greenleaf; it accommodated up to 500 guests and later burned to the ground on August 3, 1923.

THE PROFILE HOUSE, 1880s. As the tourist business increased and prospered in the White Mountains, the accommodations improved and additions to the hotels became necessary. Thus, in 1865, a number of summer cottages were added to the property and were eventually built adjacent to the hotel to house the many visitors coming to the notch. Because of the large increase in business—occasioned in part by the construction of a narrow-gauge railroad between the Profile House and Bethlehem in 1881—the old hotel was regarded as inadequate and was torn down to be replaced by the New Profile House in 1906. The new Profile House burned in 1923.

WALKS AND DRIVES NEAR THE PROFILE HOUSE, c. 1870s. A quiet solitude prevailed along the country road where visitors could reminisce and reflect in peace.

MOONLIGHT IN THE WHITE MOUNTAINS, c. 1880s. Even during the winter months, many would return to the peaceful serenity of the isolated mountain inns.

63

ECHO LAKE, FRANCONIA NOTCH, C. 1870S. One of the nearest of the many wonderful natural attractions clustered in the tiny glen of Franconia Notch is Echo Lake. It is a small but lovely sheet of water shut in on every side by towering, forest-clad hills, from whose somber sides a shout brings back wonderfully varied echoes. Starr King said that toward evening, the lake was worth visiting more for the echoes of color than of sound.

ECHO LAKE, C. 1870S. Echo Lake, a bright, 28-acre, mountain lake 1,940 feet above sea level, lies beneath the sheer granite walls and purple ledges of Eagle Cliff, which rises 1,500 feet above the lake. The lake is environed on the north and east by low, rocky Bald Mountain and Artist Bluff, on the south by Eagle Cliff, and on the west by massive Profile (Cannon) Mountain.

ECHO LAKE, FRANCONIA NOTCH, c. 1870s. On the shore of Echo Lake, this secluded retreat was nestled in the wilderness of the shore of the headwaters to the Pemigewasset River in Franconia Notch.

THE FLUME HOUSE IN FRANCONIA NOTCH, c. 1870s. A little more than 5 miles from the Profile House down the Franconia Notch was the Flume House, with room for 150 guests. From one side, the Arcadian scenery of the Pemigewasset Valley stretches away in a vista that is a full ten leagues long. From the front, the forest-clad peaks of the Franconia Range can be seen. The beautiful contrast between these two views, the rich peace of the lowland, and the sublimity of the closely surrounding mountains, gave a continual charm and refreshment to the summer visitors.

THE POOL, C. 1870S. One-half mile east of the Flume House is a great pothole that is 50 feet deep. One-hundred-foot ledges rise above it with alpine flowers and delicate ferns growing on the rocky terraces of the steep black cliffs. Pictured is a group of vacationers, dressed in their Sunday best, enjoying a stroll through the woods by the rocky shore of the Pool.

THE POOL AT THE FOOT OF THE STAIRS, FRANCONIA NOTCH, C. 1880S. This romantic moment in a rowboat is spent with a man known as "the Philosopher" and his lady. To many, he was considered the hermit at the Pool.

THE POOL, C. 1880s. A restful picnic is the bill of fare on the shore of the Pool.

SEEN FROM BELOW THE CHASM, C. 1880s. The Pool seems to be the perfect spot for gathering friends.

THE POOL. This view looks south from below the chasm into the wilderness forest of the Pemigewasset Valley, *c.* 1870s.

THE POOL, LOOKING UP THE FALLS, c. 1870s. Within the Pemigewasset wilderness resides the tranquil waters and the falls of the Pool at the Flume.

68

THE FALLS AND THE POOL AT THE FLUME, C. 1870s. At the upper end of the Flume are the rushing waters that feed into the Pool below.

THE POOL, c. 1870s. This distant view shows the Pool and the falls at the Flume in Franconia Notch.

THE POOL AT DUSK, c. 1870s. These people take one last moment with nature before returning to the city.

THE BASIN, C. 1870S. In geological terms, the basin is a giant pothole drilled in the Conway granite by the swirling waters of a melting glacier. To cut a single pothole, hundreds of stones must have dropped into the cavity, spinning and grinding smaller ones against the granite wall until they washed out or were reduced to sand. The granite crystallized deep down in the earth, the overlying material was slowly removed by erosion, and the relief of pressure caused horizontal fractures in the granite, which appear conspicuously in the Basin.

THE BASIN, C. 1870S.
The pothole is another Pemigewasset River bypass, just 1.5 miles up the notch, where the pellucid waters of the juvenile Merrimack River are gathered in a huge granite bowl.

TO THE FLUME IN FRANCONIA NOTCH, C. 1869. The greatest wonder at the southern gateway of the Franconia Notch is the deep and narrow canyon that has been eaten by a mountain brook in the coarse granite ledges near the base of Mount Flume. The location is less than a mile from the once famed Flume House. The Flume was first discovered in 1808 by Aunt Jess, the wife of Irish farmer Dave Guernsey. It is said that Aunt Jess, who was 93 at the time, accidentally found the gorge while she was looking for a lost cow. This chasm, over 700 feet in length and 11 to 24 feet in width, has 60- to 70-foot perpendicular walls rising on both sides.

THE FLUME ABOVE THE BOULDER, C. 1870. An enormous boulder used to hang between the walls of the Flume. This block of granite, weighing many tons, was doubtless dropped by a glacier during the Ice Age. This massive boulder eventually fell into the stream below during a storm and flood on June 20, 1883. After the weather cleared, the boulder was gone. Examination of the walls of the Flume showed that the water had risen to an unheard-of height and succeeded in washing this massive rock downstream. It was later discovered resting a short distance below the gorge.

THE FLUME AND A VIEW THE HANGING BOULDER, C. 1870S. It is written that the avalanche of water that swept the boulder away lengthened and deepened the chasm, eventually adding two new waterfalls to its attraction.

THE FLUME BELOW THE BOULDER, C. 1870S. Upon close examination, we find that the Flume gorge walls, eroded in Conway granite, were formed in ancient geological time. At a later period, dark molten lava from below filled a great crack and smaller side cracks in the granite, solidifying to form dikes.

73

LOOKING UP THE FLUME FROM UNDER THE BOULDER, C. 1870S. As time passed, the main dike was worn away, leaving the Flume gorge, which in time was further widened by frost and water action. In a few places, marked by signs, the remnants of the main lava dike are preserved in the bed of the gorge. Small branches or offshoots can be seen along the canyon walls.

ANOTHER VIEW OF THE FLUME BELOW THE BOULDER, C. 1870S. Stepping from rock to rock, we traverse a pathway mounted by crude steps. The pathway crosses from side to side of the ravine, and the primitive bridges bend underfoot. We finally climb the rocks again until we arrive at the massive boulder just ahead in the gorge.

A VIEW OF THE FLUME LOOKING UP INTO THE CHASM, C. 1870S. At the base of the chasm, a mountain brook dashes down among the rocky fragments, skirted by an easy plank walkway.

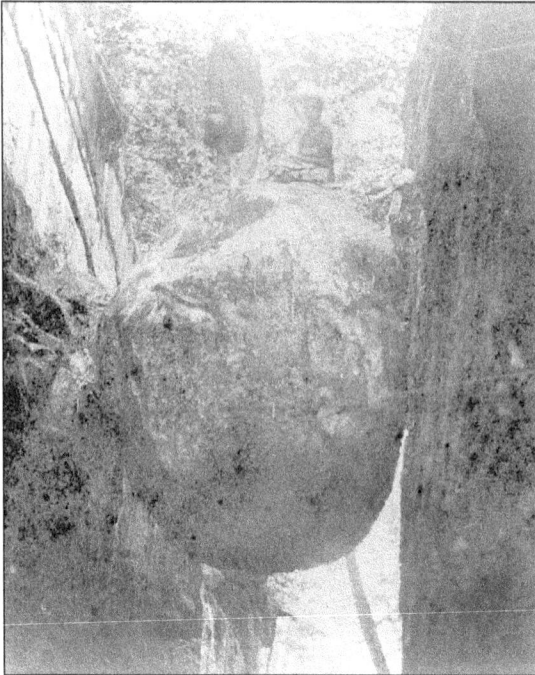

THE BOULDER IN THE FLUME, c. 1876. Proudly sitting on top of the handing boulder is Mr. and Mrs. Nathaniel S. Drake of Pittsfield, New Hampshire.

THE FLUME INTERIOR, c. 1870s. Notice the raw landscape with the high black walls as they frame the distant boulder that tightly braces the interior.

TWO LADIES RESTING IN THE FLUME, C. 1870s. Before continuing the ascent along the planked walkway, a moment of rest is well deserved.

THE FLUME WITH VISITORS WALKING THROUGH THE INTERIOR, C. 1870s. The crude walkway of planks allows the visitors to navigate slowly along the base of the canyon.

THE FLUME WITH THE BOULDER DURING THE WINTER, c. 1870s. This view looks down into the deep gorge in the dead of winter.

THE FLUME DURING THE WINTER, c. 1870s. Ice crystals form quickly on the walls, creating a scene more startling than any that the summer could offer. Starr King describes this scene: "The waterfalls were voiceless—for their fountains were changed to mines of sunless crystal now, or by the curdling winds—like brazen wings which clanged along the mountain's marble brow—warped into adamantine fretwork, hung and filled with frozen light the chasm below."

78

THE FLUME IN OCTOBER, c. 1870s. Late in the fall, ice begins to form on the sides of the Flume, as is shown by the long sheets cascading down the right side of the gorge.

A WINTER VIEW OF THE FLUME, c. 1870s. As winter sets in, thick ice sheets build up along the gorge walls, and the Flume gradually surrenders itself to the bitter winter. Soon, the entire landscape will be engulfed by ice and snow.

79

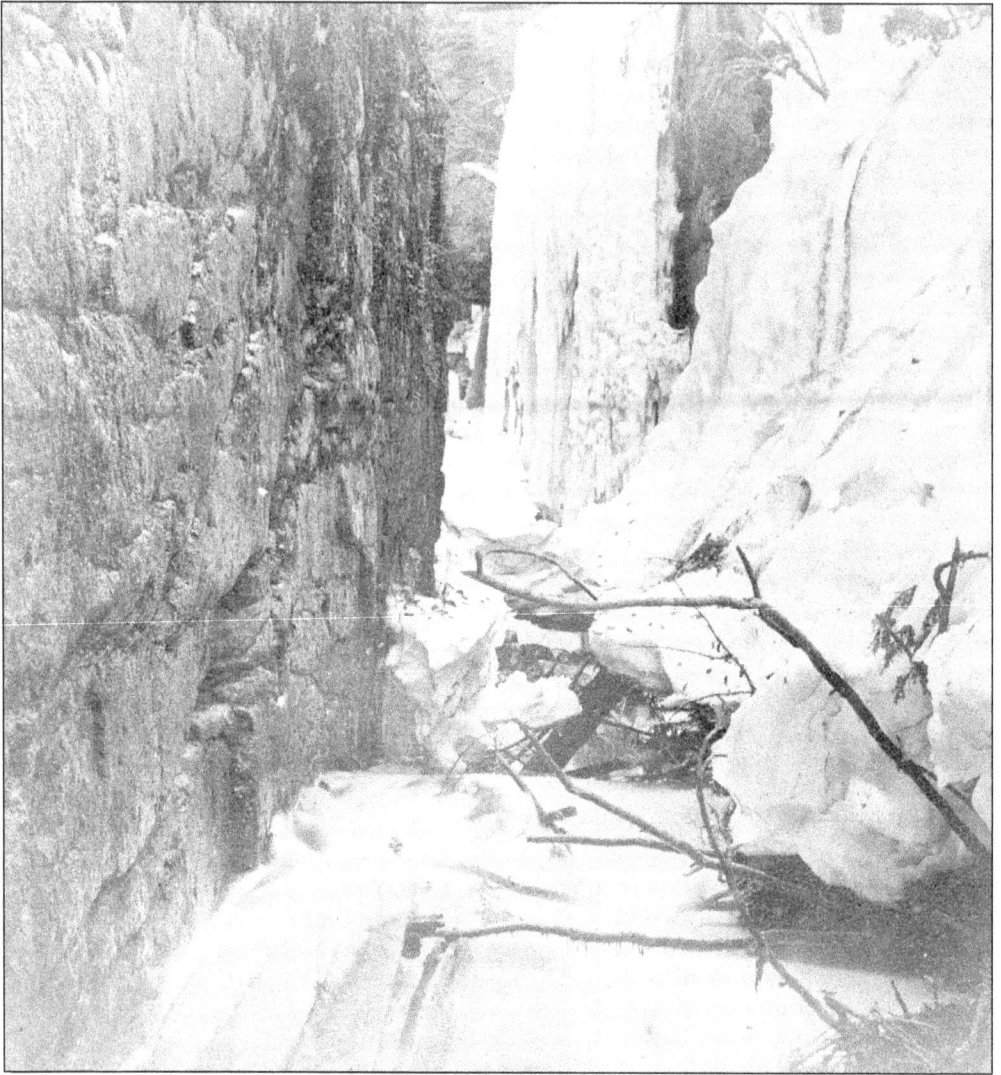

A VIEW OF THE FLUME IN APRIL. This photograph was taken on April 29, 1869. In the early spring, a thaw slowly opens the gorge, and once again a rushing cascade begins its annual run through the Flume.

Four

COUNTRY SCENES
AROUND THE MOUNTAINS
AND LAKES

MAIN STREET IN BETHLEHEM, NEW HAMPSHIRE, C. 1870s. This summer resort reputedly owes its development to an accident. It is said that in 1863, Gov. Henry Howard of Rhode Island was on a journey in this section of the White Mountains. As the coach was descending Mount Agassiz, it overturned, with serious injuries to some of the occupants. The travelers remained some weeks in Bethlehem, until the injured people had been restored to health. During this time, Howard became enamored with the beauty of the area. He made extensive purchases of land, formed a company to develop it, and provided money for establishing summer hotels. The fact that this region is favorable for victims of hay fever was discovered later, and Bethlehem became the headquarters of the American Hay Fever Association.

MAIN STREET IN BETHLEHEM, NEW HAMPSHIRE, LOOKING WEST, C. 1870S. This street stretches for 2 miles in an almost straight line from east to west along the northern slope of Mount Agassiz as it slips down into the wide Ammonoosuc Valley. The majority of its 30 hotels of all shapes, sizes, and social status line the street. In every direction are magnificent mountain views encompassing the horizon of the town. Mount Agassiz rises with the beautiful broad Ammonoosuc Valley and the Dalton Range and Green Mountains of Vermont as a background.

MAIN STREET IN BETHLEHEM, NEW HAMPSHIRE, LOOKING EAST, C. 1870S. The charm of Bethlehem has drawn a wide variety of people to this mountain community. In August 1869, President Grant is reported to have taken what was probably the wildest ride of his life, from Bethlehem to the Profile House in Franconia Notch. Road conditions were far from ideal and even with expert driving, it was supposed to take about two hours. However, with the best horses available and driven by expert Edmund Cox, who prided himself on his speed, the ride was completed in the record time of 58 minutes. The next Christmas, President Grant is said to have sent Cox a fine driving whip.

A VIEW FROM THE SINCLAIR HOUSE IN BETHLEHEM, NEW HAMPSHIRE, C. 1870S. Due to the proximity to scenic attractions in the White Mountains, the resort hotels became an important retreat for the city folk. Bethlehem Street provided one of the most impressive outlooks of the Presidential Range through its situation at "the artistic distance, giving the mountains magnificent effects under the lights of morning and evening." From the western end of Bethlehem Street, there is a fine view at sunset.

A FARMHOUSE (LOOKOFF HOTEL) IN SUGAR HILL, NEW HAMPSHIRE, C. 1880S. Sugar Hill, so named because of the groves of sugar maples on its summit, offers a delightful view of the Franconia Mountain Range that can be seen from foundation to turret just beyond the deep trench of the valley. From the Lookoff Hotel, this prospect is one of the grandest in the whole region, comprising views of both the White and Franconia Mountains.

THE VILLAGE OF LITTLETON, NEW HAMPSHIRE, C. 1880S. This mountain hamlet lies peacefully along a natural shelf above the Ammonoosuc River. This town was first granted under the name of Chiswick after an old English parish. In 1764, the term of this grant were not completely fulfilled and the charter was revoked. The town was regranted in 1770 under the name of Apthorp, in honor of a friend of Governor Wentworth. The town of Apthorp, including the major part of what is Dalton, was divided in 1784 into two townships by the two men who owned most of the land, Moses Little and Tristram Dalton, and the two towns were named for them. Littleton was incorporated in 1784.

A SCHOOLHOUSE IN LITTLETON, NEW HAMPSHIRE, C. 1880S. In this view looking north on the hill from the Main Street is the house of learning, the pride and joy of the community.

84

THE THAYLER'S HOUSE IN LITTLETON, NEW HAMPSHIRE, c. 1880s. This striking mid-Victorian-style hotel in the center of Littleton has long been the focus of social life since its opening in 1850. In the 1890s, this fashionable hotel, owned and operated by H.L. Thayer & Son, accommodated 100 people at $3 per day.

THE TWIN MOUNTAIN HOUSE, TWIN MOUNTAINS, NEW HAMPSHIRE, c. 1870s. At the Twin Mountain House, the beautiful Ammonoosuc Valley opens its wide horizon to its many visitors and guests. Surrounding the area are the North Twin Mountains, Mount Garfield, Mount Lafayette, and (down in the valley) Mount Agassiz and Mount Cleveland. This house went the way of many grand hotels; it was torn down in the early 1950s. President Grant used to stay here. The Reverend Henry Ward Beecher packed them in every Sunday, first in the hotel's ballroom, later in tents, pitched nearby to accommodate the overflow crowd of the faithful who came in large numbers to hear him preach.

THE PEMIGEWASSET HOUSE, PLYMOUTH, NEW HAMPSHIRE, C. 1870S. This house was also the station for the BC & M Railroad. There are numerous "gateways" to the White Mountains, but none are more attractive than the valley of the "Winding Water among the Mountain Pines," which is the interpretation of the Native American name for the Pemigewasset Valley. In 1850, the BC & M completed the road to Plymouth from Concord. In 1858, the BC & M leased the White Mountain Railroad, thus continuing the road from Plymouth to Littleton.

ANOTHER VIEW OF THE PEMIGEWASSET HOUSE, PLYMOUTH, NEW HAMPSHIRE, C. 1870S. The first structure was built c. 1863 by John E. Lyon, president of the BC & M Railroad. When the Pemigewasset House burned, the railroad rebuilt it, making it accessible from the station by a flight of stairs. During his visits to the White Mountains, Nathaniel Hawthorne often stopped here. He died there on May 18, 1864, in room No. 9. In 1909, the Pemigewasset House burned and was rebuilt again, this time on Highland Street in the spot where the present Pemigewasset Hall, a dormitory for Plymouth State College, now stands.

THE INTERIOR DINING ROOM OF THE PEMIGEWASSET HOUSE AND RAILROAD STATION, PLYMOUTH, NEW HAMPSHIRE, C. 1870. Daily lunch and dinner were offered to its patrons. Meals included the freshest fruit and vegetables available.

PLYMOUTH VILLAGE AS SEEN FROM THE SOUTH. This gateway village to the Pemigewasset Valley encompasses a wide interval of meadows through which a river with the same name runs. It has long been attractive to artists because the river and valley lead the eye up to superb peaks. Between the peaks is the depression that marks the site of Franconia Notch.

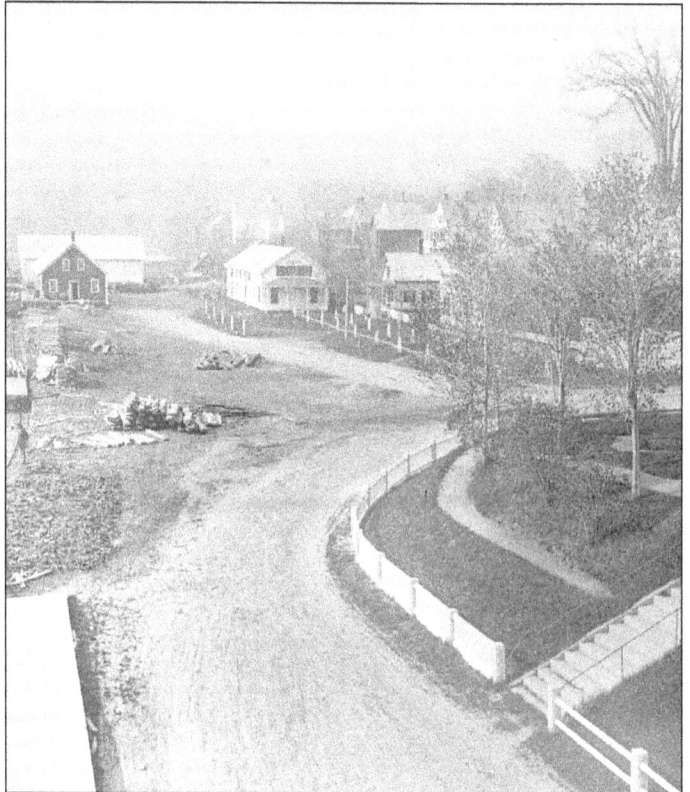

A VIEW OF PLYMOUTH VILLAGE LOOKING SOUTH FROM THE PEMIGEWASSET HOUSE, PLYMOUTH, NEW HAMPSHIRE, C. 1870S. Since 1765, industry has played an important part in local life of the community. Lumber mills, a veneer plant, a pig mill, a mattress factory, glove industries, and the manufacture of sporting goods have, at various times, been important features of village activity. Today, however, it is Plymouth State College of the University System of New Hampshire that attracts thousands of students from New England and many states on the East Coast.

RUSSELL SQUARE, MAIN STREET AND THE "COMMON," PLYMOUTH, NEW HAMPSHIRE, C. 1870S. Pictured is a portion of the downtown commercial center known to many as Russell Square, or the Common. The village had unpaved streets and gas lamps; a row of wooden buildings framed the Common with its bandstand for concerts in the center of the green.

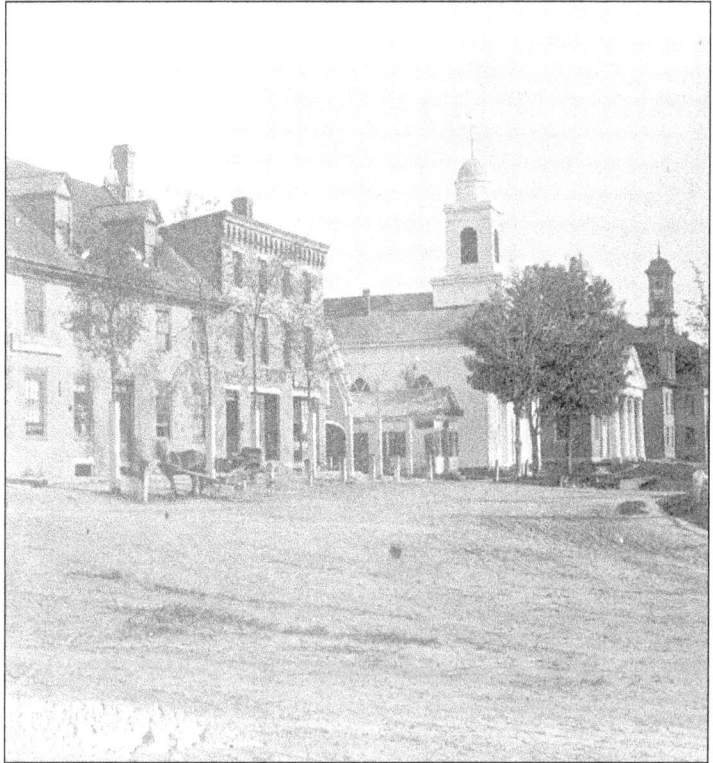

THE OLD COURTHOUSE IN PLYMOUTH, NEW HAMPSHIRE, WHERE DANIEL WEBSTER MADE HIS FIRST PLEA, C. 1870S. This small one-story frame building was an early courthouse, formerly standing on Main Street. In it, Daniel Webster made his first plea before a jury in 1805, when he undertook the defense of a murderer. It is said that the man's guilt was so evident that Webster spent most of his time attacking capital punishment. Webster lost the case.

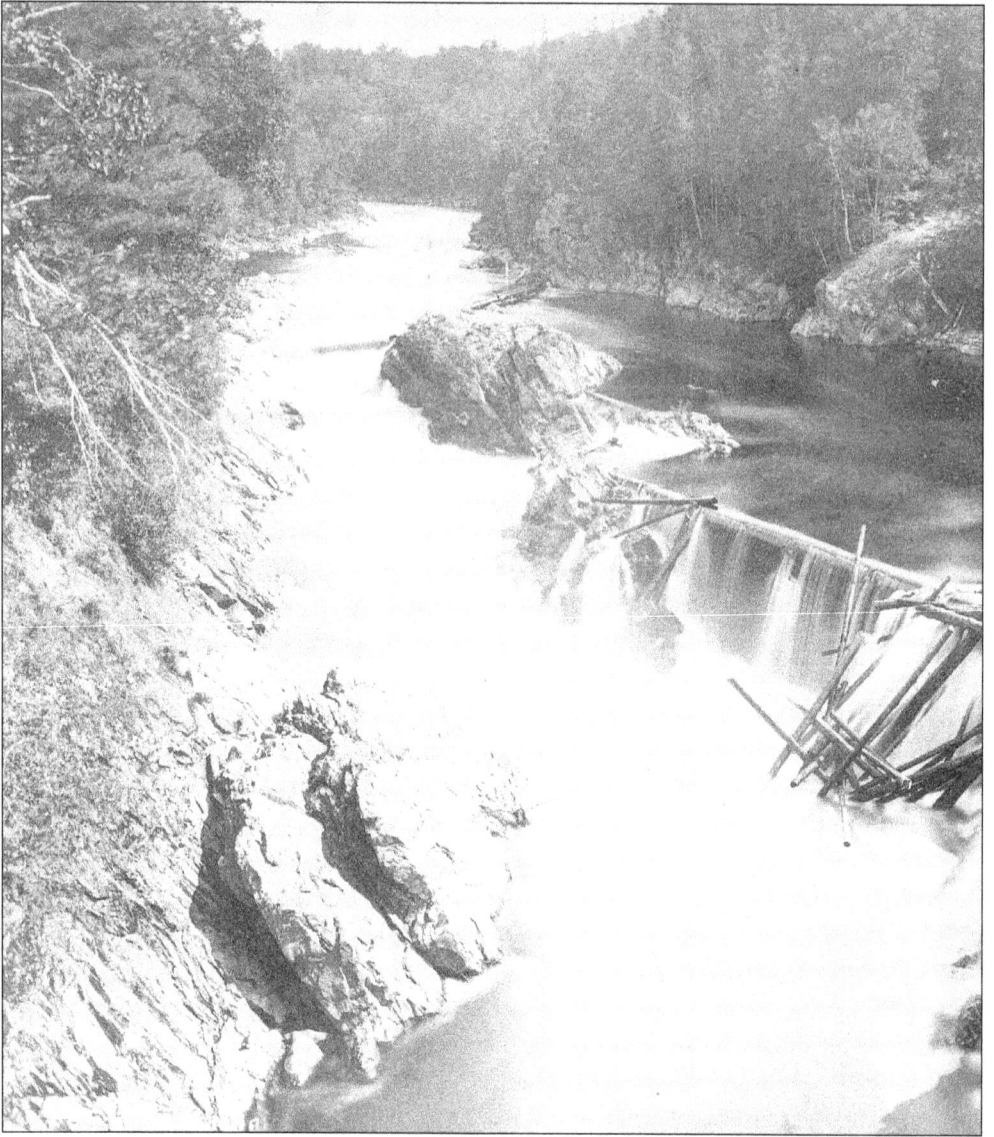

LIVERMORE FALLS, PLYMOUTH, NEW HAMPSHIRE, C. 1870S. Logging was a major industry in the area, and many sawmills dotted the shores of most waterways throughout the lakes and mountains of New Hampshire. This spot is most admired by the anglers for trout. Also, some of the most beautiful specimens of land-locked salmon can be caught at these falls.

ANOTHER VIEW OF
LIVERMORE FALLS,
PLYMOUTH, NEW
HAMPSHIRE,
c. 1870s. Looking
north up the
Pemigewasset River,
this view appears
tranquil. After heavy
rains, however,
torrents of water
can make this river
very dangerous, and
flooding often occurs.

LIVERMORE BRIDGE,
CAMPTON, NEW
HAMPSHIRE, AUGUST
10, 1874. In the
1850s, the White
Mountain Railroad
constructed this
bridge across the
Pemigewasset River.
It connected Littleton
with Plymouth. In
1858, the BC & M
leased the White
Mountain Railroad,
thus continuing the
road from Plymouth
to Littleton.

CAMPTON VILLAGE, CAMPTON, NEW HAMPSHIRE, C. 1870S. This small village was first granted with Rumney in 1761, to Capt. Jarvis Spencer. It derived its name from the fact that the surveyors of the original grant camped on this spot while running the original lines. Settlement was made here in 1765, and the town was incorporated in 1767.

BLACK MOUNTAIN FROM CAMPTON VILLAGE, NEW HAMPSHIRE, C. 1870S. Campton and West Campton were, in the 19th century, favorite spots with artists who found many subjects of special beauty in the river, meadow, and mountain scenery.

WARREN, NEW HAMPSHIRE, C. 1875. Nestled in the hills south of Mount Moosilauke lies the quiet village of Warren. The town was granted in 1764, taking its name from a remarkable seafaring gentleman from New York named Peter Warren. In 1745, he led a fleet of ships in the capture of Louisbourg, Nova Scotia, a stronghold of the French.

MOOSILAUKE MOUNTAIN FROM WARREN, NEW HAMPSHIRE, c. 1870s. This is one of the most formidable of the outlying foothills of the White Mountains. By itself, it is a mighty spectacle, rising with great power from the ranks of its own flanking highlands and pushing its way skyward. But its greatest power lies in the range of view to be had from its summit. The view is comparable only to that from the summit of Mount Washington. From this mountain, we get all forms of grandeur and beauty.

NANCY'S BROOK AND BRIDGE, C. 1870S. It is written that young Nancy Barton became engaged to a young gentleman at her farm, but after leaving him her entire dowry, he abandoned her. Determined to find him, she followed him to the notch in the middle of the winter and discovered a campfire site, cold and deserted. She continued her search until she became exhausted and fell beside the brook. A group of men from Jackson went in search of her and found her frozen body in the snow. Her lover heard of her death and reportedly went insane, dying a few years later. Tradition has it that her spirit still lingers in this valley.

THE GOODRICH FALLS, JACKSON, NEW HAMPSHIRE, C. 1870S. Here, the impressive Ellis River cascades over an 80-foot precipice into an eddying pool below. A better vantage point of this spectacle is from the point below the falls that can be reached by a path from the northern side of the river.

94

THE GOODRICH FALLS, c. 1870s. This is considered the largest perpendicular waterfall in the White Mountains. It is located about a mile from Jackson, toward the Glen Station. The view of the water coming down between the steep wooded banks is exceedingly picturesque.

A BIRD'S-EYE VIEW OF COLEBROOK VILLAGE, NEW HAMPSHIRE, c. 1880s. This northern village is situated on broad fields at the confluence of the Mohawk and Connecticut Rivers. Surrounded by low hills, it borrows its greatest scenic glory from Mount Monadnock, across the Connecticut River in Vermont, bearing a conspicuous scar left by former gold-mining operations. Its wide tree-lined main street is a gathering place for shoppers from surrounding towns in the North Country. This town was first granted with Stewartstown and Columbia in 1770 to Sir George Colebrook, Sir James Cockburn, John Stuart, and John Nelson. In 1796, it was incorporated under the name Colebrook.

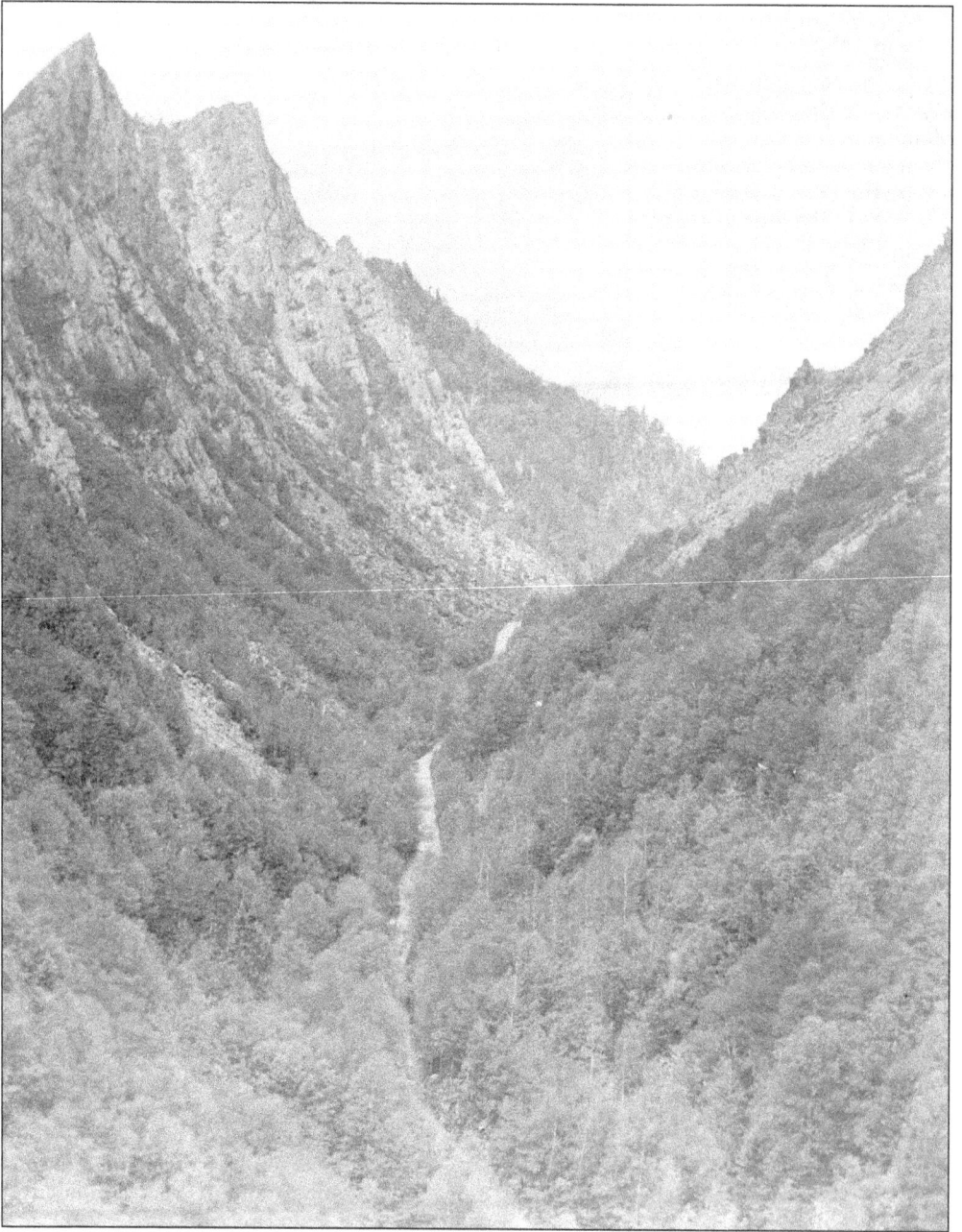

THE PASS OF THE DIXVILLE NOTCH, NEW HAMPSHIRE, C. 1870S. In 1804, a 10-mile-long road was opened from Colebrook through Dixville Notch, making the market at Portland much more accessible. No other two miles in the state surpass Dixville Notch, with its alpine ruggedness. It has been described by the *American Guide Series: New Hampshire*, 1938, as follows: "In general it may be said that the Notch looks as if it had been produced by a convulsion of nature, which broke the mountain ridge from underneath, throwing the strata of rocks up into the air, and letting them fall in all directions. The result is that the lines of stratification in the solid part of the hills point upward, sometimes perpendicularly, and several pinnacles of rock, like the falling spires of cathedrals, stand out against the sky."

A VIEW FROM COLUMNAR HEIGHTS, DIXVILLE NOTCH, NEW HAMPSHIRE, C. 1870S. The notch is a narrow pass through which an excellent roadway runs. The road threads between towering cliffs, where the geologic formations speak plainly of the natural cataclysm that forced them apart and thrust them so perpendicularly into the sky. An easily discernible profile lies at full length along one of the cliffs, in which a wild flume lies but a few steps from the roadside. The profile seen on the cliff is sometimes called by the name of Daniel Webster, although it may be difficult to trace its resemblance to this distinguished son of New Hampshire.

THE FIRST GLIMPSE OF THE GLEN HOUSE IN PINKHAM NOTCH, NEW HAMPSHIRE, C. 1870S. Many visitors considered this house as the Alpine Hotel of the North Country. Hardly had Pinkham Notch been opened for travel before John Bellows began an inn here in 1852. It was later sold to J.M. Thompson, who gave it the name of the Glen House. Two years later, it came into the hands of Charles and Weston F. Milliken, who enlarged it extensively.

THE GLEN HOUSE FROM THE BASE OF MOUNT WASHINGTON, PINKHAM NOTCH, NEW HAMPSHIRE, C. 1880S. The Glen House was the starting point for increasing numbers of visitors who drove up the Carriage Road to the summit of Mount Washington. This hotel was destroyed in 1884. However, another Glen House was built, which in its day was a model of luxury and convenience. This hostelry was a popular place from 1885 to 1893. It, too, was a victim of fire.

THE GLEN HOUSE WITH MANY TOURISTS ARRIVING FOR THE SEASON, PINKHAM NOTCH, NEW HAMPSHIRE, C. 1880s. From the Glen House is an impressive view of the Presidential Range, including Mounts Washington, Jefferson, Adams, and Madison. The Glen House was located at the junction with the Mount Washington Carriage Road and Route 16.

THE GLEN HOUSE DRAWING ROOM, C. 1880s. Elegance and refinement for guests was the first order of the day.

THE EMERALD POOL NEAR THE GLEN HOUSE, PINKHAM NOTCH, NEW HAMPSHIRE, c. 1880s. Close to the Glen House is Emerald Pool, a lull in the boisterous Peabody River, where after a cascade, the river drops into a pool as though to rest beneath the trees for a time in its rapid downward course. This spot was made famous by Albert Bierstadt's painting of the same name.

A View of the White
Mountains near the
Glen House, Pinkham
Notch, New Hampshire,
c. 1880s. A short distance
from the hotel, Mount Clay
is visible between Mounts
Washington and Jefferson.

The Cathedral Ledge,
Altitude of 1,159 Feet,
North Conway, New
Hampshire, c. 1880s. This
ledge received its name
from the cathedral-like arch
formed by the cliff. At the
foot of the ledge is a small
cave known as the Devil's
Den. From here, there is a
steep dirt road to the top of
Cathedral Ledge.

THE OSSIPEE FALLS, OSSIPEE, NEW HAMPSHIRE, c. 1880s. Located in the Ossipee Mountain Park, an area in the Ossipee Mountain Range, this waterfall is a much visited attraction in the Lakes Region of New Hampshire.

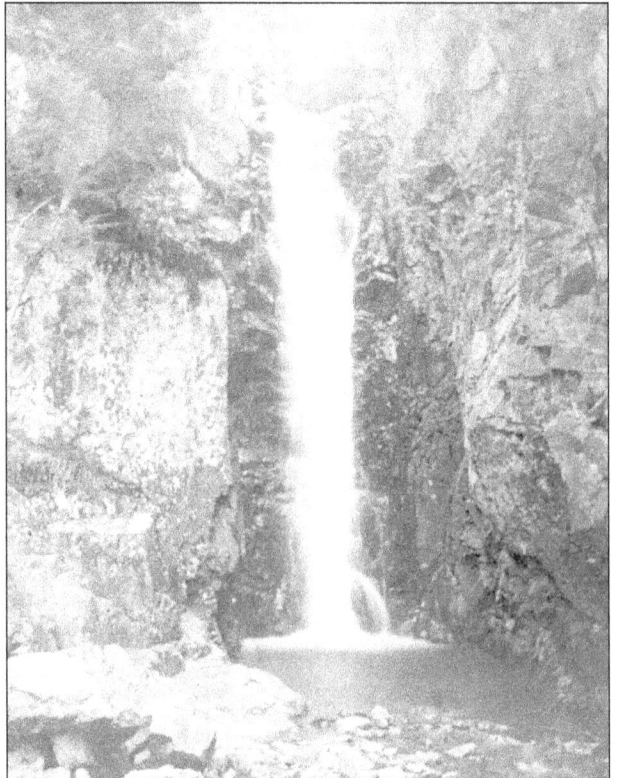

THE OSSIPEE FALLS, THE OSSIPEE MOUNTAIN RANGE, c. 1880s. This lovely waterfall is one of the most secluded and charming places in the Lakes Region. It is here that a visitor, gazing over this vast and beautiful panorama, would be inspired to repeat, with the poet of the mountains, this verse:

Over the hills to climb and flee,
And let no heart be braver.
And when they arise, like the
waves of the sea,
O like a bird of the sea to be,
Over the hills forever!
—Witter Bynner

THE CENTER HOUSE, CENTER HARBOR, NEW HAMPSHIRE, c. 1890s. This stately hotel was built in 1888, overlooking the northern tip of Lake Winnipesaukee. It consisted of three floors and two covered verandahs, one on the lake side and another facing the hills and mountains due north. Included on the premises were the main dining and serving rooms, a children's dining room, a drawing room, a music room, a ladies' writing room, a reading room, and a smoking room. There were 91 bedrooms, many of which were furnished with fireplaces. The name of the hotel was later changed to the Colonial, which was eventually destroyed by fire on June 20, 1919.

CENTER HARBOR FROM LAKE WINNIPESAUKEE, c. 1890s. Located on the northern tip of Lake Winnipesaukee, Center Harbor has a commanding view of the lake and mountains surrounding it on the east and south. During its early years, when it was apparently known as Senter Harbor, the village was an important halfway station for stagecoaches running between Concord, New Hampshire, and Fryeburg, Maine. This community was incorporated in 1797. Today, Center Harbor is very popular with seasonal visitors.

LAKE WINNIPESAUKEE WITH THE SIDEWHEELER MOUNT WASHINGTON AT THE TOWN DOCK AND RED HILL IN THE DISTANCE, C. 1880S. With it passengers, steamers plied the waters to and from this port town, not just to caress the placid waters of the lake, but also to allow visitors to leave the boat and climb Red Hill, where they could enjoy the wide vista of both Squam Lake and Winnipesaukee at the same time.

LAKE WINNIPESAUKEE FROM HORN'S CLEARING ON THE SIDE OF RED HILL, C. 1880S. The whole chain of mountains is seen several miles away as we look up the lake. Its varied charm and splendor are accented by the borders of the hundreds of islands that dot the mirrored waters.

104

STEAMBOAT LANDING,
NEW HAMPSHIRE,
c. 1880s. This landing
was located in
Center Harbor.

STEAMBOAT LANDING, NEW HAMPSHIRE, c. 1880s. This landing was located in Center Harbor.

BOATING ALONG THE SHORE OF LAKE WINNIPISEOGEE (WINNIPESAUKEE) IN CENTER HARBOR, NEW HAMPSHIRE, c. 1880s. The quiet of the water and hills seem to have the quality of still ecstasy. It is only the inland waters that can suggest and inspire such rest.

CENTER HARBOR AND THE OSSIPEE MOUNTAIN RANGE IN THE DISTANCE, C. 1880S. Here, the mountains retreat gradually back from the lake and village. This vista commands large spaces of cheerful light and a symmetrical beauty.

SQUAM LAKE FROM SUNSET HILL IN CENTER HARBOR, NEW HAMPSHIRE, C. 1880S. The limpid purity of the water and the grandeur of the adjacent mountains combine to make this rich and fascinating panorama. The lake's Native American name is said to have been either *Wonnassquamauke*, meaning "the beautiful surrounded-by-water place," or *Keeseehunknipee*, meaning "the goose lake of the highlands." It is surrounded by high, green hills. It drains not into neighboring Lake Winnipesaukee, but into the Pemigewasset River. Twenty-six islands dot its surface.

LAKE WINNIPESAUKEE LOOKING SOUTHEAST FROM ABOVE CENTER HARBOR VILLAGE, c. 1890s. This lake is a wonderful inland sea. Clustered around its shores and upon the islands, which diversify its surface, are some of the most charming of all New England's summer resorts. However, its most impressive role is found in the great panorama that stretches from the lake to all the peaks and groups in the White Mountain chain.

WOLFEBORO BAY LOOKING EAST TO WOLFEBOROUGH VILLAGE, NEW HAMPSHIRE, c. 1880s. Looking across the bay is the town of Wolfeboro, where in 1764, Col. Gov. John Wentworth completed a province road from Portsmouth to Wolfeborough. The establishment of his summer home gives Wolfeboro just claim to the distinction of being the oldest summer resort in America.

THE *FOXY* WITH THE
MOUNT WASHINGTON IN
THE DISTANCE AT WEIRS
BEACH, NEW HAMPSHIRE,
c. 1950. This 42-foot
wooden craft, owned by
Carl and Amie Wallace,
operated out of Paugus
Bay, where Burger King
is presently located.
The craft made daily
excursions from Lakeport
to the Weirs. From the
Weirs, it sailed among the
Forty Islands to Glendale,
then under Governor's
Bridge, back to the Weirs,
and finally to Lakeport,
its home port. In the
distance is the *Mount
Washington* as she makes
her final approach to the
Weirs dock.

THE *MOUNT WASHINGTON* AT
WEIRS BEACH, NEW HAMPSHIRE,
1950. The *Mount Washington*
is shown waiting to begin her
summer season. The sign on the
dock reads, "Leaves at 9:00 and
returns at 2:00 daily. A 4 hour
trip—$2.00, children half fare."
The vessel now known as the
Mount Washington was built on
Lake Champlain and operated
under the name *Chateaugay* as a
sidewheeler between Burlington,
Vermont, and Plattsburgh,
New York. In 1940, she was
purchased from the Champlain
Transportation Company.
The vessel was dismantled
at Burlington, cut into 20
sections, loaded on freight cars,
and shipped to Lakeport, New
Hampshire. There, she was
reassembled, fitted with steam
engines, and christened the
steamboat *Mount Washington II*
to replace the old *Mount* that was
destroyed by fire in 1939.

Five

REFLECTIVE MOMENTS AND FAMILY TIME BY THE LAKES AND STREAMS

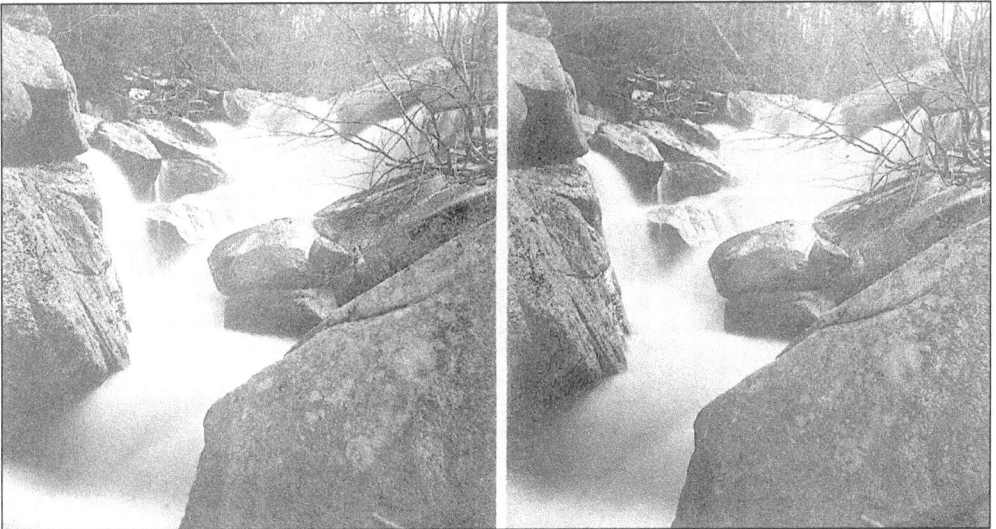

A RUSHING MOUNTAIN STREAM, C. 1890S. During the spring, thousands of cold mountain streams rush wildly to the river, where they finally join the open waters of the Atlantic.

THE *UNCLE SAM* AND THE *MOUNT WASHINGTON* DOCKED AT THE WEIRS, NEW HAMPSHIRE, 1950. The third mail boat on Lake Winnipesaukee was known as the *Uncle Sam* and was built in 1906. The craft, a single-screw vessel, was 65 feet long, had a 14-foot beam, drew 7 feet of water, and was capable of carrying 100 passengers. In 1945, she was converted from the traditional steam to the new diesel-type engine. She kept her franchise on the lake until 1961, when she was retired. The mail service continues today via the *Sophie C.* Docked beside the *Uncle Sam*, we may see the aft end of the *Mount Washington*. Note that the fantail section of the vessel is open, and that the ship had no third deck at this time. Today, the entire aft section is enclosed, and a third deck has been added for passengers.

SECLUDED WATERS IN THE
PEMIGEWASSET WILDERNESS,
c. 1870s. During the summer,
these mountain waters quiet
themselves and flow peacefully
into the ocean.

THE FIRST
SNOWSCAPE,
c. 1870s. There is
nothing more tranquil
than the first snow
as it carpets the fall
landscape to make us
aware of the
oncoming winter.

111

A COUNTRY FARM IN THE WINTER, c. 1870s. Secluded in the depth of winter near Cannon Mountain, this country farmhouse will always have a warm hearth for its neighbors and visitors.

A VILLAGE IN WINTER AFTER THE BIG STORM, c. 1890s. This restful hamlet in the valley sleeps peacefully while Mother Nature does her seasonal duty.

A CENTER HARBOR
BOAT HOUSE ON LAKE
WINNIPESAUKEE,
c. 1890s. Clustered
along the shoreline are
many of these quaint
boathouses, boasting
the new powered
steamers that soon
plied the waters.

CAMPTON, NEW HAMPSHIRE, C. 1890s. Young men relax at the falls on the Pemigewasset River.

A LOGGING MILL BY THE SIDE OF THE LAKE, c. 1870s. Spotted along the shoreline of the lakes and ponds were hundreds of these mills, waiting patiently for the next load of logs to arrive.

PICNIC TIME IN THE PASTURE NEAR CHOCORUA LAKE WITH MOUNT CHOCORUA IN THE DISTANCE. These three ladies are having a restful time by the fence, with their serving women standing by patiently.

THE FARMER'S
HOME, C. 1880S.
The entire family
joins in the industry
of cutting the cords
of firewood for their
winter supply.

THE OWL'S HEAD, JEFFERSON,
NEW HAMPSHIRE. This slide
occurred in the morning on
July 10, 1885, during a heavy
thunder shower, accompanied
by a terrific rushing and
roaring that was heard for
several miles. Oscar Stanley's
house and barn were entirely
demolished. His stock and a
large portion of his farm were
buried in its course. He and
several men barely escaped
with their lives, one of whom,
Don J. Walker, died of his
injuries soon afterward. In
about four minutes from its
start, the slide reached its
terminus—a distance of more
than 2 miles—having swept
the earth, trees, and rocks to
the depth of 50 to 100 feet and
a width varying from 50 to 400
feet. It much exceeds the noted
Willey slide and will long be a
prominent point of interest for
White Mountain tourists.

115

THE BROOK KEDRON FALLS IN THE CRAWFORD NOTCH, C. 1880s. This cascade from Mount Willey is one of many tributaries that flow into the valley and finally to the Saco River. The brook, cascade, and falls are located a short distance from the Willey House on Route 302.

THE SILVER CASCADE, CRAWFORD NOTCH, C. 1880S. This beautiful cascade on Webster Mountain is one of the most admired of the White Mountain spectacles. Much of its 1,000-foot course is made in long slides over the smooth ledges; these reaches are succeeded by short perpendicular leaps over steep rocks.

A Yankee Doodle Parade, c. 1880s. On this day of frolic, fun, and patriotism, these young boys have the right spirit.

A Rally around the Flag, 1891. Our young people remind us to celebrate Flag Day.

THE MERRIEST DAY OF ALL THE YEAR IN NORTH CONWAY, 1892. Main Street in North Conway, New Hampshire, is where all gather to celebrate—the occasion does not matter.

THE GLEN ELLIS FALLS, WHITE MOUNTAINS, NEW HAMPSHIRE, C. 1860–1862. The falls, about 4 miles south of the Glen House on the North Conway Road, are reached by a quarter-mile walk from the highway. The main waterfall, which descends through a deep groove worn in the rocks, is 70 feet in height and is considered by many to be the finest in the White Mountains. These falls are located on the Ellis River at the base of Wildcat Mountain, the formidable ridges of which tower to great heights. The origin of the name is not known; however, the Sweetser guide notes that Ellis may have been originally spelled "Elise" or "Elis."

DIANA'S BATH, NORTH CONWAY, NEW HAMPSHIRE, c. 1870s. Gently flowing over a table of granite, terminated by a beautiful waterfall some 10 feet in height, the stream plunges into a great number of holes (or basins) worn smooth by the action of the water. The largest of these—sparkling in the sunlight or quiet in the shadow—seems indeed to be the bath that a goddess might use.

A PICNIC GATHERING BY THE FALLS ON OSSIPEE MOUNTAIN, c. 1870s. Family picnics with friends on Sunday afternoons were popular pastimes in the mountains during the vacation months.

THE FALLS OF THE AMMONOOSUC IN THE WHITE MOUNTAINS, c. 1880s. The stream descends over rapids and falls from nearly 50 feet through a narrow gorge with walls of polished granite ledges. Below the plunge, the water whirls in white and billowy masses through a sinuous chasm between massive cliffs.

THE FALLS OF THE AMMONOOSUC IN THE WHITE MOUNTAINS, c. 1880s. The headwaters of this river flow off Mount Washington through the Ammonoosuc Ravine and finally merge with the Connecticut River in Woodsville, New Hampshire. The river falls nearly 6,000 feet from its origin at the Lakes of the Clouds, just below the summit of Mount Washington. *Ammonoosuc* is an Abenaki word meaning "fish place."

122

PUDDING POND WITH MOUNT KEARSARGE IN THE DISTANCE, c. 1880s. A quiet mountain pond was never far from the grand hotels where visitors could enjoy the soft symphony of nature's music.

STONY BROOK IN THORNTON, NEW HAMPSHIRE, c. 1890s. Stony Brook is one of the many tributaries that flow into the Pemigewasset River.

123

A FAMILY GATHERING IN CENTER HARBOR VILLAGE, C. 1890s. With the Colonial Hotel in the background, this quiet setting was ideal for a friendly photograph.

A YARD SALE, C. 1870s. This yard sale was located by a country inn in the White Mountains.

124

WHITEFIELD, NEW HAMPSHIRE, C. 1880S. Children pose on this hill in Whitefield.

CAMPTON, NEW HAMPSHIRE, C. 1880S. Some Conway boys attended this camp in Campton.

A Sunday Stroll in Center Harbor Village, c. 1870s. This day calls for the top hat, white gloves, and that special lady for a Sunday stroll.

THE TROUT FARM, MEREDITH, NEW HAMPSHIRE, C. 1900. This farm was operated by the Meredith and Lake Winnipesaukee Association Fish Hatchery.

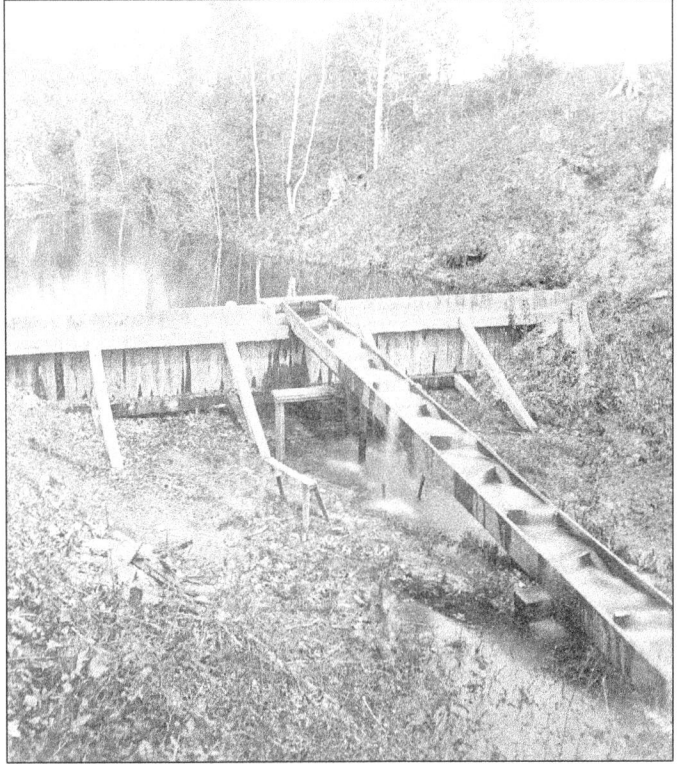

ENGLISH JACK'S CASTLE, CRAWFORD NOTCH, NEW HAMPSHIRE, C. 1880. Many old-timers remembered English Jack as "the Crawford Notch Hermit." He was a very colorful mountain character who built his dwelling just above the "Gate of the Notch" in the late 1870s. Tourists enjoyed his entertaining storytelling. He will be remembered.

127

THE OLD ABONDONED GRISTMILL, C. 1870S. Many abandoned mills are now left to Mother Nature's mercy. We may find them adjacent to the old country road, in the backwoods of old homesteads, and in the wilderness in the Pemigewasset Valley. Wherever they are, they remind us of the early industry of years past—a memory not to be forgotten.

www.ingramcontent.com/pod-product-compliance
Lightning Source LLC
Chambersburg PA
CBHW080908100426
42812CB00007B/2211